PRAISE FOR *CULTIVATE*

"*Cultivate* is delightful and breathes grace through every page. Lara gives inspiration to nurture life through the seasons in which we find ourselves. Reading this book will make you feel that you have a personal friend standing by your side to give you encouragement to live your life well."

SALLY CLARKSON
BESTSELLING AUTHOR OF *OWN YOUR LIFE*, *THE LIFEGIVING HOME*, AND *DIFFERENT*

"*Cultivate* is rich soil for the soul! Whether you are a new sprout, just beginning to brave life in the light; a tender shoot fighting for space among rocks and weeds; or a mature plant in need of nurture and pruning, this book will help you thrive. With her characteristic honesty, humility, and patience, Lara Casey uses her spiritual 'green thumb' to gently nudge us toward an intentional life of godliness and growth. Scriptures and stories from Lara's own spiritual journey inspire us to self-reflection without self-sabotage and progress without perfection. Journal prompts and reflection questions help to demystify the growth process and break it down into manageable steps. If you are ready for a new season of spiritual growth, dig into *Cultivate* and get ready to bloom!"

ELIZABETH LAING THOMPSON
AUTHOR OF *WHEN GOD SAYS "WAIT"*

"Lara's commitment to growth, in both her personal life and in business, has long inspired me. To lead an authentic life, we must look inward for answers. In the pages of *Cultivate*, she candidly shares her triumphs and failures, and her secrets to success for growing a purpose-filled life. What an incredible gift to the world!"

ERIN BENZAKEIN
FARMER-FLORIST AT FLORETFLOWERS.COM
AUTHOR OF *CUT FLOWER GARDEN*

"I loved *Cultivate*. Through these pages, we learn to embrace the season we're in: when to get our hands dirty, when to rest, when to prune, and when to wait. Lara shows us through examples and actionable steps that the best things—whether that's a garden of colorful zinnias or an intentional life focused on what truly matters most—are not created all at once, but through the little-by-little."

INDIA HILL
TWENTYSOMETHING WRITER AT BOOKSANDBIGHAIR.COM

"Are you exhausted, weary, or worn out from trying to keep it all together? *Cultivate* is a life-giving read that invites you to pause and choose a different path. Lara's authentic voice will encourage you to let go and embrace the messiness of a truly abundant life. You'll be refreshed and ready to step toward an intentional life rooted in what matters most."

EMILY ENOCKSON
RELUCTANT FARM GIRL AND SERVANT LEADER AT ZACHARIAH'S ACRES

"This book will help you know about God and growing things. I like the part about the butterflies and bees."

GRACE ISAACSON
AGE 5

CULTIVATE

ALSO BY LARA CASEY

Make It Happen: Surrender Your Fear.
Take the Leap. Live on Purpose.

CULTIVATE

A Grace-Filled Guide to Growing an Intentional Life

LARA CASEY

THOMAS NELSON
Since 1798

Published in Nashville, Tennessee, by W Publishing, an imprint of Thomas Nelson.

Thomas Nelson titles may be purchased in bulk for educational, business, fund-raising, or sales promotional use. For information, please e-mail SpecialMarkets@ThomasNelson.com.

ISBN 978-0-7180-2166-5 (TP)
ISBN 978-0-7180-2167-2 (eBook)

Library of Congress Cataloging-in-Publication Data

Library of Congress Control Number: 2017935761

Printed in the United States of America

17 18 19 20 21   LSC   10 9 8 7 6 5 4 3 2 1

For my little gardeners:
Gracie, Joshua, and Sarah

I love you from my head tomatoes.

God lives in every garden,
He loves each growing thing.
Forget your ills,
Get out and dig and sing.

CONTENTS

PART 3: SAVOR THE FRUIT

WELCOME TO THE THICK OF IT

Before we get started, you should know something: I am an unlikely gardener. My grandfather could grow tomatoes with his eyes closed, but I never seemed to get it.

For most of my life I craved instant results and quick fixes. I wanted flourishing and full bloom right from the start.

I preferred to skip the in-between part. The sometimes-awkward waiting, tending, and growing part.

So it's no surprise that I've killed a lot of plants in my life.

Several years ago, during a long season of marriage challenges, I bought an orchid for my desk, thinking the colorful blooms would help me feel something other than despair. But within days, my poor little plant was withered and dying.

That orchid represented my life at the time. My soil was dry and depleted, and I desperately needed sustenance.

My husband, Ari, and I met at the gym, back in another lifetime when I was a personal trainer and he was in the navy. We got married five months later in Las Vegas. (Typing that never ceases to make me feel a little shocked at my own story!) We had both gone through painful relationship endings shortly before we met. Neither of us was in a great place to start a new relationship, much less a serious one. But we fell for each other quickly, and when it came time for him to move to a new base across the country, we had to make a choice: Do we say goodbye or take a huge leap of faith together? We chose the latter and eloped.

When the honeymoon phase ended, reality hit. We come from different faith backgrounds. Our hurried courtship and differences caused a lot of tension in our first years together. We became two ships passing in the night and even started sleeping in separate beds.

I tried to fill my emptiness by throwing myself into building a business. I worked hard trying to grow something that would fill the broken places in my life, trying to prove my worth, hoping that once I did it all, once I had it all, and once I finally got it all done, I would finally feel content.

But having it all done, all together, and checked off never happened. Instead, my feelings of being overwhelmed grew like weeds.

LOOKING GOOD ON THE OUTSIDE

Fixing the root of my emptiness felt completely out of my control, so I tried dozens of surface solutions.

Searching for a more organized life, I bought new planners and pens.

Seeking lasting joy, I loaded my shelves with books that promised formulas for quick-fix happiness.

Maybe getting fit would solve everything, so I purchased running shoes and a gym membership.

Perhaps more creativity would be the thing that brought me contentment, so I loaded up my cart with blank canvases and craft supplies.

I felt emotionally drained, so I reached for comfort food and social media.

I bought a journal, thinking it would help me slow down and be more introspective.

I acquired cookbooks, clothes, subscriptions, and throw pillows.

But I learned that it was going to take a lot more than throw pillows to heal the mess in my heart. No matter how many things I purchased, my life still felt empty.

CULTIVATE IT

Can you relate? What surface solutions have you tried lately?

In rare moments of stillness, when I let myself actually feel what was below the surface instead of running from it, I felt shame.

Shame for being so busy.

Shame for not having close friendships.

Shame for spending long hours at work at the expense of my well-being.

Shame for being the editor-in-chief of a wedding magazine when my own marriage was in ruins.

Shame for withholding my talents, dismissing them as useless since I wasn't an expert.

Shame for the state of my soul.

MAKE A CHOICE

I feel tenderness in sharing this with you. I think back to who I was then, and I feel for her. That Lara didn't know any better. She was trying to make something of her life. She hustled hard, despite often feeling hopeless. She was doing what she thought she had to do: Trying to pay the bills. Trying to hear God's voice in all the noise. Trying not to give up on her marriage. She was trying. But she couldn't see at the time that there was another way forward—a much better way.

If changing your life feels impossible and you're tempted to close this book in search of new throw pillows like I was, take heart. Life *can* change. You can move forward on an entirely new path. And here's the best part: You don't have to do it all, be it all, or check it all off to experience change. You don't have to do any of this on your own, or perfectly, for the course of your life to be radically redirected.

How do I know? My life has been transformed since those hustle-hard days, and my prayer is that these pages—and my story—will help you know and live the truth: no matter how far gone or far away from blooming you feel, new life is possible.

I don't know your current situation or what's going on in your heart, but I know that there is grace—God's transforming gift of new life—for your heartache, your restlessness, and whatever it is that's keeping you from flourishing. There isn't a mess you've made that God can't make into something new and beautiful.

A NEW WAY OF LIVING

Like my life at the time, the orchid on my desk seemed beyond saving. I hid it out of sight in a corner of our bathroom, where it lived for four years, getting watered maybe once every couple of months. In fact, I almost threw it away.

But one morning I stared at the dying plant and got frustrated—mad, even. I was mad at the emptiness I felt and frustrated that nothing I was doing was working. Sometimes frustration can spur us to action, though, doing things we never thought we would do.

I thought changing the direction of my life would take a monumental effort on my part, like a grand strike of lightning, but for me it was a surprisingly small spark that illuminated a new path.

When anything is exposed by the light, it becomes visible, for anything that becomes visible is light.

—EPHESIANS 5:13-14

Every fiber of me was tired of feeling like I was constantly fumbling in the dark. I was tired of living in a way that wasn't really living at all.

I was tired of quick fixes that didn't fix anything.

I was tired of living in a state of lack—lack of time, lack of peace, lack of confidence, and lack of meaningful connections with people.

I was tired of working hard but feeling like it wasn't getting me anywhere that mattered.

I needed a new way of living, from the ground up.

When we are faced with something that isn't working, we get two choices: stay where we are, or redirect and consider a new way forward. Staying isn't bad. Waiting can be fruitful. But sometimes we stay where we are because of fear, don't we? I have often wrestled with this. My need for nourishment and change felt so dire at the time that I was genuinely afraid to consider anything but immediate remedies. How could I wait for water to come when I felt so parched? How could I heal the pain in our marriage in time to save it? It felt too big. Too impossible for me.

I wanted a fast fix, but God wanted my heart. I took a leap of faith to consider a new, outside-of-my-comfort-zone path forward.

What I'm about to tell you may seem elementary, but for me this was a revolutionary mind shift: I thought about the big picture. Where did I want to be when I was eighty years old? What would be important to me then, and what wouldn't? Considering these questions was like someone slowly turning the lights on. I started to see a new way forward. It wasn't a path I had ever taken before, but what I was doing wasn't working. It was time to do the opposite of what I had been doing!

Instead of living for the short term and patching things to just get by, I thought about the long term.

I committed to little-by-little progress instead of the all-at-once.

I started to cultivate.

Starting with my little plant. In my frustration one day, I pulled that orchid out from the dark corner, put it by the light on the windowsill, and started to tend to it. I watered, fertilized, repotted, pruned, and watched my withered orchid for any signs of life. I had no idea what I was doing. It was a haphazard process, but God was changing something in me.

I kept coming back to the little pot on the light-bathed

windowsill, despite the perpetually lifeless, brown leaves. They remained unmoved, it seemed, by my visits. But every time I tended to that shell of a plant, watering and tending with expectant hope, God was changing me—opening me to believe in something I couldn't yet see.

BLOOMING LOVE LETTERS FROM GOD

Despite my imperfect care over the course of two years, one morning I saw a flush of green in the orchid's pot. I took the plant outside in the daylight to be sure my eyes weren't deceiving me.

There it was.

My little plant was alive!

That flush of color grew to two hearty, green leaves. Soon after, a stalk emerged—and weeks later, flower buds.

I held the pot in my hands and cried. This wasn't about a plant; this was about my life. I had been addicted to instant gratification, searching for contentment in whatever was easy and fast. But easy and fast didn't bring this plant back to life, nor did my own plans or strength. My orchid had flourished only with careful and consistent tending, little-by-little progress, and trusting God to make it grow in His timing.

The day the flower buds unfurled, I ran around the house in celebration. Where there once had been doubt, hope was now blooming before me in shades of pink and golden yellow.

And you know what's amazing? Right now, as I type this to you, almost a decade later, that same orchid is keeping me company on the dining room table. Its twelve flowers are like little blooming love letters from God.

CULTIVATE IT

What in your life needs to be revived or given a fresh start?

Tending my dried-up orchid over and over again for two years—and seeing God use those little steps to make new life happen—gave me a peek into how He works. There was something to the process of taking small, intentional steps forward, embracing imperfect progress along with oceans of God's grace. I was discovering an essential truth: good things didn't grow all at once but rather little by little.

Little by little, God was changing my life. He was showing me real grace: an invitation to experience new life in my brokenness and undeserved forgiveness in my mess. He transformed my marriage, my well-being, and my soul with this essential grace—not a hall-pass or an excuse for missteps, but my imperfect life exchanged for Jesus' perfect one, my fruitless striving for His life-giving power, my weakness for His strength, and darkness for light.

People often ask me how I stay so motivated and energized. I could tell you I try to eat healthy foods and sleep well at night, but the real answer is grace.

His grace took two people who were going nowhere and set us on a path to somewhere.

That motivates me more than any coffee or accomplishment ever could. And it's this essential grace that gives me the freedom to cultivate—embracing little-by-little, imperfect progress, because I know I don't have to be perfect to grow what matters alongside Him. Grace motivates me to try, to plant, to grow, and to take leaps of faith, not because I have to but because I want to. His life-giving grace made me a cultivator, right where I was, flaws and all.

I wasn't sure if there was any hope for my parched life. But new life gradually began to grow. Although I had many doubts, I discovered that doubts are doorways. When we lean into our doubts, seeking truth where we feel restless and unsure, God leads us to greater faith, and sometimes to unexpected new paths.

As I will share with you in the pages ahead, that resurrected plant inspired me to start a garden. (Typing those words still blows me away.) As I cultivated my garden, faltering step by step, God taught me how to cultivate an intentional life too—right where I am, in every season.

The lessons I learned in the dirt changed everything for me—my faith, my work, my family, and my future—and the same can happen for you.

EMBRACE THE TENSION

Welcome to the thick of it, where it's beautiful and messy and fueled by grace. Imagine me with you, wherever you are reading this, looking you in the eyes to tell you what I know now: a flourishing life is possible, no perfection required. In fact, it's in the imperfect—the dirt—where things grow. Not despite the mess and tension, but right smack in the middle of it.

In the parts of your life that feel dry, lifeless, and messy.

In your weakness.

In your broken places.

In your hard conversations.

In your fears and failures.

In do-overs and boo-boo kisses.

In *I love you* and *I'm sorry.*

In leaning into what feels unkempt.

In deciding that done is good enough.

Even in that thing that you haven't told a soul, that feels too ugly and painful to admit.

I'm learning that there is magic in the middle ground. There's good stuff for us in the tension of the in-between. Growth happens in the wait.

In what feels awkward and unbalanced, growth and life are happening.

I'm still in the thick of it most days. I'm imperfect, yet I'm cultivating an intentional life.

And I know God isn't done with me yet.

BECOME A CULTIVATOR

Mankind's first job was to cultivate and keep a garden (Gen. 2:15). God could have given us any number of tasks to do or places to be, but He is the author of intentionality. This first assignment was a meaningful foundation. Perhaps He put us in the garden to teach us something essential.

The Hebrew word used for "cultivate" in Genesis is the same word translated "serve" in Joshua 24:15: "As for me and my house, we will serve the LORD." Cultivating an intentional life is about serving the Lord for His purposes and growing what matters with Him.

CULTIVATE IT

One of the following definitions of *cultivate* may stand out to you more than the others. Circle or underline words or phrases that jump out to you most.

To *cultivate* means to

- serve,
- nurture,
- nourish,
- prepare,
- encourage,
- improve,
- refine,
- pay attention,
- foster growth,
- loosen and break up hard ground, and
- care for what you've been given.

What words or phrases stood out to you most in that list? *Pay attention* leaped off the page at me. In the dark days of my marriage, I had been paying attention to things that didn't matter, giving them importance with the currency of my heart and time. But why?

DO YOU NEGLECT OR NURTURE?

So often we want to cultivate an intentional life, but something is in the way. What do you feel has been holding you back lately?

CULTIVATE IT

Mark the words that grab you most in the following list.

The opposite of cultivating is

- abandoning,
- neglecting,
- disorganizing,
- destroying, or
- ignoring.

As I looked over the words in this list, *neglecting* hit me hard. That's exactly what I had been doing in my life. I had neglected my marriage, my well-being, my relationships, and my soul because they seemed too hard to fix with my own strength. Making a purchase? I could do that. Replying to e-mails? I could do that. Dreaming up projects that would help grow my business? Yes, I could do that. But mending my heart, pulling my soul out of the pit, and finding time for rest? Those things felt out of my control. I nurtured only what I thought I could control.

CULTIVATE IT

What areas of your life feel neglected?

What have you been choosing to nurture instead, and why?

Sometimes choosing a new path, or one that requires great faith, isn't easy. Maybe it's hard to imagine living a different way in your current circumstances. But what if doing the hard thing, taking a risk, or stepping into the uncomfortable will change everything? What if giving up something will open space for something much better? Cultivating what matters is worth every bit of what we give up in time, pride, money, possessions, status, or comfort.

I have to pause here to tell you something: I don't know your story or where these words will meet you, but as I write these pages, I am praying for you. Maybe we know each other in real life, or maybe we don't yet, but we share something: we want to do this life well. And perhaps you are beginning to realize, as I did, there's some junk in the way, such as fear, bitterness, worry, or a pull toward wanting instant gratification and quick fixes. You are wondering when you will finally feel like you're really *living*.

I am fighting tears as I type this, because I needed someone to pray for me during those uncultivated days. I felt alone. I didn't know how to ask for prayer or where to start. My faith felt broken and distant and imperfect. I needed something bigger than I am to help untangle the mess and give me a fresh start. I needed a way to sift through all the things to get to the only thing that matters: His truth.

REPLACE LIES WITH TRUTH

In the pages that follow, we are going to uncover ten common lies that keep us from flourishing:

Lie #1: I have to do it all.

Lie #2: I have to be perfect.

Lie #3: My life needs to look like everyone else's.

Lie #4: It's impossible to start fresh or move forward.

Lie #5: I have to know all the details of the path ahead.

Lie #6: Waiting is not good or productive.

Lie #7: Small steps don't make a difference.

Lie #8: I will be content when I have it all.

Lie #9: I can do life by myself.

Lie #10: The past isn't valuable; it's all about the future.

CULTIVATE IT

Which of these lies above have you caught yourself believing? Circle the lie(s) that stand out to you.

What other lies are holding you back from cultivating an intentional life? (Examples include: *I'm not good enough*; *It's too late for anything to change*; etc.)

As we break up these lies and replace them with truths, good things will have fresh, new space to grow in your life. Are you ready to dig in? I am!

HOW TO USE THIS GUIDE

This is not a reading-only book. Just as gardens don't grow simply by thinking about them, cultivating an intentional life takes some digging and doing.

Gardening requires lots of water—most of it in the form of perspiration.

—LOU ERICKSON

Write It

As you read these pages, I encourage you to journal your thoughts in the margins and in the "Cultivate It" prompts. If the word *journal* makes you cringe a little, you're in good company. I don't love journaling either, but I do love the feeling of getting tangled thoughts out of my head so I can create margin for the meaningful.

Your "journaling" can be half sentences, chicken scratch, or just a jumble of words. My handwriting is as all over the place as my thoughts are, so my journaling looks . . . well, messy! Practice getting your hands dirty as you interact with this content and respond to the "Cultivate It" prompts throughout each chapter.

Dig In

Each prompt and question in these pages gives you a choice: choose to keep living the lie or choose to break it up and dig into truth. That's going to take some muscle. Tilling the hard ground of winter in my garden each year leaves me sore the next morning—a good kind of sore that reminds me I woke up some muscles that had been dormant and made some progress in that dirt. New growth can come because I broke up the hard ground. The act of digging into what feels messy or broken may feel challenging or uncomfortable, but it's necessary to grow new things. The hard work of cultivating will be worth it!

Cultivating means embracing what feels awkward and undone. When you feel stuck or pressured to have the perfect answer to a question in this book or take the perfect step forward based on what you are learning, stop and remember: make a mess, and dig into what feels imperfect! It's okay to start your answers with, "I'm not sure, but here's an idea . . ." It's okay to try something that doesn't work the first time. It's okay to change your mind, pull out something that's not growing well, and start fresh again. Embracing the imperfect is essential to growing what matters.

Grow at Your Own Pace

If you follow @GraciesGarden on Instagram, you know my favorite flowers to grow are zinnias. They take a few weeks to reach full bloom, but they flower from May all the way until the first freeze in November. The days of waiting are worth the months of flowering. So take a lesson from my zinnias, and go at your own pace as you work through each "Cultivate It" prompt. Getting through each one might take some time and thought—that's okay! Slow growth is still growth. Get started today and focus on little-by-little progress, not perfection. The process will be worth it.

You have the freedom to skip the questions and prompts altogether, pick a few that stand out to you, or do them all as you go through these pages. They are just suggestions, like seeds from me to you, to try planting. If you feel overwhelmed or rushed or tense, be curious. Notice how you feel as you are challenged to go outside of your comfort zone and answer each question. Know that an intentional life isn't grown from what you do but rather by whose you are. God is with you right now and as you dig into each question.

Cultivate Together

I've created a special Cultivate Together Guide in the back of this book—a ten-week discussion guide that will equip you to cultivate what matters and grow in community. Grab your girlfriends or small group, and dig in together.

Grow with Grace

You don't have to actually grow plants as you go through this guide, but if you want to, you'll find a Cultivate Gardening 101 Guide at LaraCasey.com/cultivate. Fair warning: I've learned a thing or two about growing things over the years, but I'm no expert. Please reference page 77, "Grace from the Garden: All the Plants I've Killed," for proof.

The subtitle of this book has the word *grace* in it for a reason. No matter what mistakes you've made or will make, you don't have to rely on your own strength to grow this life. You don't have to be perfect or have it all together. God has it, and His abundant grace is yours for the taking.

IT'S TIME TO CULTIVATE

My words may be imperfect as we go through this work together, but I hope they give you the freedom to know that your words, and your life, don't have to be perfect either. I've been given a story to tell—and live—and so have you.

Let's do this.

It's time for the dry, forgotten places to be transformed.

It's time to break up the hard ground and to prepare for new growth.

It's time to embrace the mess and cultivate an intentional life.

PART 1

PREPARE YOUR GARDEN

....

CHAPTER 1

CULTIVATE WHAT MATTERS

LIE: *I have to do it all.*
TRUTH: *I can't do it all and do it well.*

I almost ran into a wall—a literal wall in my own home.

I had just had a new baby, and I struggled with balancing motherhood and business. I worried that my growing company couldn't withstand the changes that were happening in my personal life. I feared that everything would fall apart.

I felt pressure to keep it together.

I thought that everyone else had it together but me.

I believed that I had to get it all done—and done perfectly.

And, despite my efforts, the only thing that felt done was me.

Rushing to get back to my desk one morning, with a baby in one arm and reading an e-mail on my phone on the way, I came *this* close to crashing my face right into a lovely shade of Benjamin Moore's "Mindful Grey."

That wall was a wake-up call. I was trying to get it all done out of fear. And it felt painfully familiar. I had grown so much since my hustle-hard days years ago, but I found myself believing similar lies—the lies that said I had to do everything and do it all perfectly. Everything felt urgent, important, and necessary. I settled back at my desk, took a breath, and considered something I didn't want to admit: maybe all the things I thought I had to do didn't actually need to get done.

IDENTIFY WHAT YOU WANT TO CULTIVATE

Maybe you want your life to transform, but you don't know where to start. One surefire way to stay right where you are is to stay right where you are. Even if what we're about to do together feels challenging, let's do this in the name of not staying where we are. Ready?

As we begin this journey together, name the one thing that you most want to change or grow in your life. You can change or refine your answer later, but let's mark our start together.

What do you want to cultivate? As you read this right now, what's the first thing that comes to mind?

CULTIVATE IT

Below is a list of some ideas to get you started thinking about what you want to cultivate in your life. Circle the ones that fit you best, or write your own. Practice making a mess by defining your thoughts as they are right now, even if they feel imperfect or impossible.

Perhaps you want to cultivate

- A healthier lifestyle
- A stronger marriage
- A deeper faith
- Intentional connections with family
- Joy in your children
- Contentment in what you have
- More time in prayer
- Learning and education
- A new business venture
- Being more present
- Deeper friendships
- Confidence in your life path
- Creativity
- Work that allows you to use your gifts
- A life-giving home with open doors for hospitality
- Balance and rest
- _____

CULTIVATE IT

Look at the items you circled or wrote. Envision what your life would be like if you grew those things. In the margin, jot down a few words about how cultivating these things would make you, and those around you, feel.

Almost running into that wall made me want to grow breathing space—deep and wide breathing space. I had too much to do and care for. I was still trying to do all I had done before this new season of my life, but it was too much. I needed a shift.

I wanted to unrush my pace in favor of presence.

Imagine planting a peaceful garden in the middle of everything you have going on right now, right where you are. The image of a well-tended garden is a stark contrast to how we live most days, isn't it? But it's possible. In the middle of the chaos and pressure all around you, let the story I'm about to share with you give you real hope that you can cultivate a new way of thinking, being, dreaming, and doing—right where you are.

It's winter as I begin this book, and my garden beds are mostly bare except for the kale and cabbage that don't mind the cold. I still can't believe this garden is mine and that I grow things. As of this writing, this is my fifth year having a garden. *Me.* The former plant killer and dirt dodger. Every time I step out into the dirt, I'm reminded that God is the author of change. He can change anyone and anything. He has proven that time and time again in my life.

DECIDING TO START A GARDEN

So how did I go from one withered orchid to a tiny suburban farm? The way many good things grow: imperfectly.

When I was young, my Grandpa Cecil loved taking me to his vegetable garden. I'd hunt for roly-polies and snails and help him pull turnips. I spent a lot of time with my grandpa in his garden. I just wanted to be with him. You see, something about Cecil was magnetic. He had a joy and contentment that drew people in. He had been through a lot in his life, including multiple heart surgeries, great loss, and illness, but his faith rarely wavered. He knew that he couldn't take any thing or accolade or dollar bill to heaven with him, so he invested in what would last—loving God and planting good seeds in people's lives, including mine.

Sometimes God uses another person to plant a seed in our lives. And sometimes that seed doesn't sprout till decades later—right on time. I wanted to cultivate an intentional life, like Grandpa Cecil's.

As my little orchid bloomed, the rest of my life was revived too. What felt impossible happened: my marriage changed. My husband, Ari, and I went from constant turmoil and chasing all the wrong things to being given new life by God's grace. Being forgiven of the hurt we had caused each other and the mistakes we had made was unfathomable, incomprehensible, and clearly happened by the power of a very real God. We named our daughter Grace, for the gift we had been given. My wedding magazine company changed right along with my life, and we began to help couples plan not just weddings but also meaningful beginnings to married life. Our small group at church became a significant part of our lives as Ari and I grew in our faith. Ari started a new job as an assistant professor at the University of North Carolina at Chapel Hill, and we began to figure out parenthood together.

There's something about being a new parent that puts life in perspective quickly. I began questioning the way I was doing everything. How could I teach our daughter to do life well? How would the way I care for what I've been given teach her to do the same? How could I teach her that God can change what feels impossible, like He did with our marriage?

If I wanted Grace to live an intentional life, I was going to have to live one myself. That thought was overwhelming. Even though so much had changed in our lives, there was much more

I knew God wanted to grow in me. The most powerful teaching I could do with Grace would come from my own in-progress example.

I wanted to plant roots, create memories through meaningful traditions, and teach Grace about living with all five senses—living outdoors in God's creation in the same way I did as a kid. I wanted to teach her how to grow, tend, harvest, and savor the things that matter.

I did something that felt a little wild, and yet so right, and I bought a few plants: basil, oregano, and rosemary to season family meals with. I put the pots on the back steps, and Grace quickly took an interest in them. She visited them each day to smell their leaves and munch on the basil, bringing me a sprig or ten as I cooked dinner each night. Adding these plants to our family was oddly thrilling at the time. *I* bought plants. I was up to a total of five live things to tend to now: my orchid, three pots of herbs, Grace, and Ari.

But something in me craved more. I thought about Grandpa Cecil. Reflecting on his faithful, simple, content life, I got this crazy idea that I wanted to plant a garden in our side yard. I envisioned picking tomatoes from the garden for dinner and letting Grace experience the joy of growing our own fruits and vegetables. I convinced Ari of my new hobby by promising him fresh pesto and pickles. But there was far more that the garden would give us than edibles.

GARDENING WITH GRACE

Now, let's rewind a few pages and remember that I never thought I would be a gardener. I didn't know the first thing about gardening! A houseplant was one thing, but starting a garden was, for me, like a cow moseying around in a parking lot: unlikely. Gardening seemed like a gentle hobby for those who had more time on their hands. Yet here's a sentence I never thought I'd type, much less live: God was transforming a plant killer like me into a gardener.

Gardening was not a hobby I randomly picked out of thin air; it was a craving. As my life was being changed by God's grace, my hands followed. I began to feel an insatiable desire to nurture what I had been given—and even more than that, to grow things I never had imagined wanting to grow!

CHOOSING FEAR OVER FAITH

That next Saturday morning, I decided to get my garden growing. I stood in the yard and opened a pack of yellow pear tomato seeds.

As I unsealed the packet, I steadied my hands. If you've ever enjoyed an heirloom tomato in the summer, you may have noticed the seeds. They are tiny and delicate. I reached into the packet and touched one with my pointer finger. It grasped on to me, as if I now held some responsibility for its life. I could choose to cultivate it or let it remain dormant.

Inside a seed is something powerful: potential. And potential is scary, isn't it? It calls us to grow—to take action, to become, and to step forward in faith.

Lifting the fragile seed carefully out of the packet, my breathing slowed.

Planting seeds is risky. It's putting our trust in something bigger than we are. It's optimism and faith. It requires letting go, and I don't like letting go. I like being in control. I like efficiency, security, routine, and predictability. I like having a plan.

As I looked down at the seeds, I knew I held possibility in my hands.

What do I do now? How do I plant this? When is the right time to plant tomatoes? How deep in the soil do I plant them? How much should I water them? How many seeds do I plant at once? What if I don't do this perfectly and it doesn't grow?

I had a choice: risk imperfect progress to grow new life or regret not growing anything at all.

In that moment, faced with the possibilities in a tiny tomato seed, I chose fear over faith.

Yes, you read that right.

I flicked the seed off my finger back into the packet and sealed it up.

GARDENING IN WHITE PANTS

I was too afraid to plant anything from seeds at first. I feared I would mess up and everything in my garden would die. And I believed the lie that if I couldn't do it perfectly, I wasn't going to do it at all.

I was conditioned to think that messes were bad and doing it perfectly the first time was good. To me, there was no in-between.

We don't like imperfect starts, do we?

We want perfect right out of the gate.

But all plants grow through the dirt, and so do we. Making a mess doesn't mean you become one.

CULTIVATE IT

What have you been wanting to do or start, but you have been afraid of trying?

What are your fears?

Trying to cultivate an intentional life without making a mess at times is like trying to garden in white pants. I've done this—stepping out into the tomato vines, thinking I'll just pick a few things, prune a couple of rogue vines, and somehow walk away dirtless. But keeping my white pants clean isn't possible when pruning "the Bobs," as we call our tomatoes (thank you, VeggieTales). That doesn't ever happen, no matter how hard I try.

And you know what? When I'm focused on keeping my white pants dirt-free, I end up missing the joy in what the garden calls me to: being fully present right where I am. Hands, heart, mind, feet—all of me present. Embracing the imperfection gives me undistracted hands, unafraid of getting dirty and doing hard work.

The garden begs for my presence, and when I give it, it grows.

CULTIVATE IT

Have you ever felt as if you were so focused on not messing up that you missed the joy of being fully present at that moment? If so, describe the situation.

I WANT IT ALL

After my fearful encounter with the tomato seeds, I decided to try a different route to gardening.

This time I sought some help from my gardener friend Scott. I went to Scott's nursery, For Garden's Sake, and picked out seedlings instead of seeds. I chose several varieties of tomatoes and basil, dreaming of ripe tomatoes with fragrant sweet basil. And then I saw the peppers. *I love peppers!* And cucumbers, squash, melons, sweet potatoes, carrots, figs, and a beautiful Elberta peach tree. I remembered that my mom had taken us on many road trips through Elberta, Alabama, when I was a kid to get the sweetest peaches I've ever tasted. *I have to get the peach tree. And Grace would love fun herbs like pineapple sage and chocolate mint!*

"You may not have room for all of these, Lara," Scott warned as he eyed the tree and everything I had packed into my wheelbarrow. I didn't see the problem and told him I would try to fit it all in.

If I was going to do this, I wanted to do it big. I wanted the perfect garden—overflowing with all of my favorite things. I wanted the best, the biggest, and a grand start.

You probably know where this is going.

That first year of gardening, I learned a lot of lessons, as I am apt to do: the hard way. I spent that summer pruning and picking and getting a crash course in many things, including "Don't Plant Too Much in Your Garden."

I planted five different varieties of tomatoes. They grew, but they were pretty tasteless. I learned that if you grow tomato vines too close together, their roots get tangled and they start to suck the life out of each other. They needed more room in order to flourish.

If you look at someone's garden, you can tell a lot about that person. I tend to think I can handle a lot more than I actually can.

CULTIVATE IT

Do you tend to believe you can handle more than you actually can? If so, write out a few thoughts about times you've experienced this, and what happened.

THE POWER OF NO

The spring I started my garden, I was speaking at conferences, traveling, running two businesses, and consulting for small business owners while caring for Grace. I was doing good and purposeful work, but too much of a good thing can still be too much.

I was addicted to yes.

Yes, I'd love to do this project with you!

Yes, I'd be happy to write a post for your blog!

Yes, I'd love to speak at your conference!

Yes, I'd love to get together!

Yes, I'll be there!

Yes!

Come summer, I was burned out. I was tired of growing. I was worn-out trying to do it all and not doing a whole lot well.

I was tired of my overcrowded life.

I craved margin in my schedule. Time to teach Grace all the things I had hoped to teach her: A balance of meaningful work and nourishing rest. Room for physical, emotional, and spiritual self-care in order to better care for others.

I wanted to flourish as a friend, a mother, and a wife.

Something had to change, but how was I supposed to make changes when everything was already in motion?

It's simple gardening math: plants need space for roots to grow, and they need adequate nutrients. If you want them to flourish, then give them these things.

Untangling our lives can feel more complicated, though. Relationships, expectations of others, deadlines, and dates press on us and feel impossible to unravel and unrush.

So how do you do it? How do you know what to say no to when it *all* feels urgent? How do you simplify?

A powerful fertilizer to nourish the things that truly matter in life is the word *no*. We often think of *no* as a scary and disconnecting word, but it has the power to be one of the most loving and connecting words you use.

It's okay to let go, not keep up, and not do it all.

It's okay to disappoint people in favor of growing what God has given you to grow.

It's okay to say no.

We have only so much space, energy, and nutrients in our lives. I don't know about you, but I do not thrive in an overcrowded life. Whether it's too many dreams planted at once or too many social commitments, work projects, family activities, or unresolved conflicts, all those things take up space.

When I try to do it all, nothing grows well.

CULTIVATE IT

What in your life needs more room to flourish? What thing(s) could you say no to or spend less time on in order to make room?

What fears or concerns do you have about saying no to those things?

_____

There are inevitable shifts in our lives that require making room—such as a new baby, growth in a business, an illness, or changing life responsibilities. We only have a finite amount of energy, resources, and time to spend each day. When life shifts, no matter the reason, we must be willing to surrender something to make room. This is not easy, is it? But it's necessary. This is why I almost ran into that wall. I didn't want to change. I didn't want to let go at the time. I thought everything would fall apart if I didn't keep it all together. And I sat at my desk that day and I felt guilty. I felt like a bad mom and a bad business owner. I just couldn't do it all. But I've learned since then that there is no guilt needed when times of overload press in; there's just grace and an opportunity to shift. When life changes, which it often will as we grow, something has to shift, or overload occurs. If we resist the change, our lives resist us until we let go.

Pray with me:
God, help us to know when You want us to say no and what we need to let go of in order to make room for Your good fruit to grow in our lives, amen.

MAKE ROOM FOR GOOD FRUIT

Good fruit is characterized by love, joy, peace, patience, kindness, goodness, faithfulness, gentleness, and self-control (Gal.

5:22–23). But here's the thing we often miss: a life aimed at any one of these virtues will leave you chasing your tail because seeking to obtain the fruit of the Spirit isn't the goal. Cultivating a meaningful life with God is the goal, and the fruit is the result. In order to live a truly fruitful life, we must seek God above all else. He is the Master Gardener who makes our lives fruitful.

> The righteous flourish like the palm tree
>   and grow like a cedar in Lebanon.
> They are planted in the house of the LORD;
>   they flourish in the courts of our God.
>
> —PSALM 92:12-13

Think about your life and honestly evaluate how you are spending your time, energy, and focus. Are there areas of your life or activities that you know you need to let God heal, change, or strengthen to become fruitful?

CULTIVATE IT

Below is a list of areas in which we usually invest our time and hearts. Feel free to tailor the categories to fit your life. Give each category a rating between 1 and 10. A rating of 1 means this area is not fruitful at all and you wish for this area to change dramatically. A rating of 10 means you are seeing God's fruit in this area of your life.

Friends/Family
Money
Career
Spiritual Life

Health
Environment
Recreation
Relationship with a significant other

Circle the area above that needs the most changing.

Now write out some of the activities you do in each of these areas of your life and if they are helping you cultivate what matters. What specifically in each of these areas is fruitless?

Every decision we make points us in one direction or the other. The things we set our focus on can give us life or suck it out of us. We can waste our time, talents, energy, and resources, or we can ask God to help us cultivate. When we choose the latter, we open up space for His good fruit to grow.

Look at the fruitless distractions and activities on your list, then call them what they are: weeds. Weeds drain the nutrients and life out of what you want to grow.

Weeds can be tricky, though, because you can't just lop them off on the surface of the soil—you have to pull them out from the roots. If you don't, they will come back in multiples. Maybe the roots of what's keeping your life from producing fruit can be pulled out rather easily, or maybe they run deep. I've had to take a shovel to some unruly crabgrass that tried to take up residence in my rutabagas. Perhaps there is something that you need to turn over to God to heal like unresolved conflict, unhealthy habits, or a broken heart. Or maybe there's something in your schedule you need to let go of. Yes, I believe in finishing what you start if the Lord tells you to, but maybe

He's trying to tell you that that project, activity, or pursuit served its purpose, and now it's time to move forward. Maybe it's time to let go of something. When we say no to one thing, we're saying yes to something else. Maybe your creative gifts don't have to be turned into a business; they just need to be used. Or maybe you should finally make room in your life to do that thing you've always wanted to do, because it's going to prepare you for what's next. And maybe what's next is really good!

CULTIVATE IT

Looking over all you have identified so far, what is one weed that you know you need to pull?

You may have a lot of weeds on your list, but gardening teaches us an essential life skill: doing one thing at a time. I cannot multitask in the garden. Each task requires both hands and my full attention—especially weeding. Starting with just one weed will give you courage and momentum to get rid of many more. Weeds are bound to pop up, but cultivators learn over time how to deal with them swiftly and effectively. Choose one distraction you will pull, one activity you will say no to, or something that needs to end, starting now.

Whatever you need to pull out of your life to give your everything to God, don't waste another second. But there is such a thing as overpruning. As you pull the weeds and prune your time, remember that true faith in God is about a relationship, not about rules. It's easy to look at our lives and see all the things we perceive we are doing wrong, prune those out, and miss the point. We can be so focused on creating a weed-free garden that we miss the big picture: the garden itself. When I do this, I live out of a place of restriction, rather than flourishing in grace and freedom.

CHOOSE CULTIVATING OVER KEEPING UP

Gracie loves being outside. She collects sticks and makes castles, draws in the dirt, and sifts through rocks and garden treasures. One afternoon she was happily playing putt-putt with pebbles and fallen birch branches. I stood in the yard with her, and I felt the familiar pull of my hand reaching into my pocket for my phone—as if my hand were magnetized to it. It was almost mindless, a muscle memory from trying to get ahead in every moment I could. But I stopped myself. This trying-to-do-it-all compulsion was sucking the life out of me, and it was time to pull that weed right out of the ground. I pulled my hand out of my pocket and reached for the twig I had just stepped on instead.

"Grace, I found another stick—a really good one!" You would have thought I had found an ice-cream-cone tree, she was so excited. I went over to her, got down on my knees in the dirt, and had more fun with sticks than I can express to you. It was a joy that comes from trusting God's ways over our own, in the seemingly small things and the big things too. Good fruit began to sprout.

There will always be weeds, and there is also always a way to grow what matters. An intentional life is made of not a perfect string of decisions and weed-free living but of a garden grown for His glory, no matter how many times you mess up or how many times those weeds pop up along the way. Now, don't look too into this next sentence as a metaphor, but in my garden, having lots of weeds just means you've got some good, desirable soil!

God was opening my eyes to see the weeds that had popped up almost without me noticing, as weeds are known to do. I realized how precious and fleeting my time was with Grace, and how unimportant many things were that were getting more of my attention at the time. And I made a decision: no more. I'm willing to disappoint people, delay answering messages, fall behind on e-mail, and let go of perfection in favor of cultivating a lasting love and connection with my daughter.

I choose cultivating over keeping up.

DO WHAT MATTERS

I had, indeed, started a garden. Or, rather, it had started me. The lessons I learned in the dirt seized me whole.

I still can't do it all, but now I don't want to. I just want to do what matters, no matter how many times I stumble along the way. The cultivated life—broken and imperfect—is far more meaningful.

Cultivators pay attention to WHAT MATTERS.

SEEDS OF GRACE AND TRUTH

We can't do it all and do it well.

A powerful fertilizer to nourish the things
that truly matter in life is the word *no*.

Too much of a good thing can still be too much.

God is the Master Gardener who makes our lives fruitful.

You don't have to do it all. If unrushing your
life feels overwhelming or impossible, consider
that it *is* impossible for you. That's why we need
God. Where you can't, He already has.

Choose cultivating over keeping up.

GRACE FROM THE GARDEN

Garden Company

Gardening boring? Never! It has surprise, tragedy, startling developments—a soap opera growing out of the ground.
—PAUL FLEISCHMAN, *SEEDFOLKS*

Gracie's Garden began as three pots of herbs—just enough rosemary, basil, and oregano to cook with. As Gracie grew, so did our garden space. Three pots turned to two small raised beds. The next year we pulled out three holly hedges, and our garden grew to seven raised beds.

Along with the expanded space came some new friends. We have lots of company in the garden. Let me introduce you.

First up: Nutty the Squirrel, also known as Señor Pumpkin Eater. Nutty has become fodder for many a bedtime story around our house, but he isn't something of fairy tales. He is a very real, seedling-loving, exceptionally sneaky eastern gray squirrel. I imagine he lives a life similar to the furry friends in Nancy Rose's *The Secret Life of Squirrels*.

Hootie, our plastic guard owl, is up next. His bright yellow eyes are beady enough to fend off most humans, but Nutty goes right on noshing on our pumpkin seedlings. Hootie has been known to escape his post and, thanks to Gracie, find new places to guard inside the walls of our home. One particular winter morning Ari and I woke up and opened our eyes—and there was Hootie on our dresser, staring at us in bed! Hootie has since been banished from the house.

The "magic trio"—the goldfinches, butterflies, and bees—love to play on my zinnias in the summer, like kids in the sprinklers. I love them so much. They flutter about together in harmony, taking turns harvesting their pick of seeds, nectar, or pollen. They are the reason I pack in as many flower seeds as I can!

Then there is our little brown bunny. Her favorite breakfast is the sweet potato vines, which is fine with us, since the sweet potato vines are as plentiful as fried chicken at a church picnic. She faithfully comes to eat at seven thirty each morning in the warmer months. But there was one night—oh, what a rough night. I pulled in the driveway after dinner out with the family, saw a flash of a little brown creature in front of the car, and heard a *thump*. I turned off the ignition and burst into tears. *My little bunny!* I leaped out of the car and ran into the house. I couldn't bear the thought of what I'd just done. Ari consoled me and offered to go check and see if the bunny was still under the car. I cried and cried as he went to check. He didn't see any sign of her. I assumed she'd hopped off, limping from her injury. I was sad for days. Devastated. Then, one morning, guess who hopped out from the blueberry bushes, with no signs of injury? Yep, our little bunny! I cried again. This is admittedly a bit embarrassing to share. I obviously inherited my mom's compassion for animals. I know our bunny did not literally die and come back to life, but in my mind she did. She reminds

41

me to tread carefully in our driveway and to believe in positive possibilities.

A favorite friend in the garden is our neighbor's cat, Ranger. He lives up to his name, keeping the garden protected from the critters that try to dig in it. The sight of his black-and-white-spotted fur darting out of the bushes to greet Grace every morning makes me very grateful. They have become quite good buddies. She tucks flowers in his collar, and he doesn't mind one bit. He brings Grace lizards and frogs as tokens of his affection. Gracie isn't so sure about his gifts, but Ranger is good company and she loves him all the same.

There is another garden companion I dare not mention, lest they decide to return. But for the sake of you getting a full picture of what Gracie's Garden is like, here you go: hornworms. Don't Google *hornworms* unless you are ready to be as grossed out as I was when I first saw them on a half-eaten tomato plant. These bright green caterpillars are hungry! They can grow up to five inches long and can consume an entire tomato plant in a week. The only way to get rid of them naturally is to pick them off by hand or purchase a swarm of parasitic wasps. Yes, I did look up how to acquire a band of mail-order wasps once. I couldn't do that to our mailman, Walter, though, so hand-picking it is! I love Gracie's Garden. I do not so much love the hornworms.

While we do try our best to ward off certain pests, we have learned to embrace the company we keep in the garden. The best kinds of gardens are cultivated not for the gardener alone but also for all who wander in. We now know to plant a few extra pumpkin seeds for Nutty and a bevy of wildflowers for the magical trio, and we don't bother to trim the sweet potato vines because of our sweet bunny.

When we cultivate an intentional life, we have plenty to share. We learn to share, not out of our excess but to purposefully grow things to bless others. We even let the hornworms munch a bit on the tomatoes.

....

CHAPTER 2

EMBRACE YOUR SEASON

LIE: I have to be PERFECT.

TRUTH: It's in the IMPERFECT that things grow.

When Grace was three years old, Ari and I found out I was pregnant again. We were extremely grateful. I looked ahead in my schedule and began canceling work events and other activities, making room for a new baby. We told our church small group the good news, and they celebrated this answered prayer with us.

Hours after making our happy announcement, I crawled in bed and a dull headache began. Cramps and pain kept me up through the night.

I didn't want to believe it was happening—but it was.

I was having a miscarriage.

In the days and weeks that followed, I didn't know what to do with myself. I wanted to stay in bed and look to distractions to try to ease my grief. I didn't want to go anywhere or talk to anyone, much less go out in the garden. I hadn't planned on planting much that spring because I thought I'd be taking care of a baby. And now the garden depressed me. It felt empty.

But God had a purpose in this time that felt lifeless and dark. Though I couldn't see it yet, I was about to begin a season of unexpected growth.

FINDING A PURPOSE IN THE PAIN

Winter turned to spring, and the smell of fresh mulch and thawing earth made me restless. I sat in the kitchen with Grace, took a deep breath, and did the hard thing: I got still. I prayed silently, *Why, Lord? I trust that You have something good in this, even though I can't feel it right now. This was not what I had planned. We prayed and hoped and trusted. Was this my fault somehow? Is there something wrong with me? Will we ever have another child? Why do I have to experience this pain? What do I do now?*

I lifted my eyes, and part of the answer was happily coloring beside me: Grace. I curled my arms around her and savored her more deeply than I ever had before. I buried my nose in her auburn curls, inhaled her sweet smell, and considered that maybe one thing I was supposed to do in this season was to love her, Ari, and others in new ways.

Maybe there was a purpose in this pain. In this blank slate. Maybe this season of grief was part of God's good plan.

For everything there is a season, and a time for every
matter under heaven:

a time to be born, and a time to die;
a time to plant, and a time to pluck up what is planted.

−ECCLESIASTES 3:1-2

Before a seed can sprout, it is placed in the ground. There in the dark, surrounded by the mess of the dirt, it begins soaking up nutrients that will eventually help it to sprout. The sprout breaks through the hard outer shell, leaves its protective covering behind, and presses through the dirt toward the light.

Seeds hold a lot of wisdom. They let go of their outer shell in order to move forward. They embrace their season, and do what they were created to do. Even when we can't see it, new life is growing beneath the surface. I couldn't see it at the time, but the days of grief following my miscarriage were a time of being transformed under the surface, in what felt bleak.

WHAT SEASON ARE YOU IN?

Before gardeners can plan what they want to grow, they consider the seasons. I don't plant seeds in the winter here in North Carolina because they will likely rot or lie dormant in the cold. I wait until spring—April 15, to be exact—after the last danger of frost, to plant anything. I've gotten overeager a time or two and planted tomatoes in March, only to have to dig them right back out of the ground and give them a temporary abode in my kitchen during a hard freeze. I've learned to honor the boundaries and wisdom of the seasons.

Likewise, when you uncover what you want to cultivate in your own life, consider what season you are in.

I don't believe it was an accident that you picked up this

book at this specific time in your life. And your path isn't an accident either. What if everything you have experienced—all the heartache and joys—has been God preparing the soil of your life for something good to grow?

Whether you are in a season of spring, summer, fall, or winter right now, your season is preparing you for the next.

And seasons change for a reason.

As much as I long for spring each year, I couldn't do two springs in a row. I would eventually become burned out by the forward motion, and I'd likely start to take new life for granted. I love the warmth of summer and being outside, but I eventually start to crave the coziness of fall. A reflective winter helps me to rest and prepare for the seasons ahead. But an endless winter would leave me longing for the fresh start of spring and new growth.

I always thought it was unattainable, this elusive thing called "balance." But as I've observed my garden over the years, I have noticed something. In the seasons, we find balance. The seasons allow my garden to rest and grow at just the right times, and it's the same with our lives. The seasons teach us how to do life well, revealing a life-giving rhythm: we flourish through intentional periods of stillness, growth, hard work, and rest. We need this rhythm in our days, in our weeks, and in our everything.

Maybe this is your season of spring, to start something new—to break ground into fresh soil. Perhaps it's your season to take a leap of faith or plant roots right where you are, blooming where you are planted.

Maybe this is your season of summer, watering more often and being watered. A time to prune and pull weeds, work hard in the heat, or tend to what matters most to you. A fruitful season of deepening your connections to community.

Maybe you are in a season of fall, ready to do the work of the harvest and count the fruit that has been growing. A season of savoring and gathering.

Maybe you are in a season of winter, waiting for spring and new life to come. You are resting, abiding, reflecting, and clinging to the hope of spring ahead. And maybe this season of waiting is your time of ripening—a season of preparation, getting you ready for something good ahead. Something far better than you expected.

Maybe it's time for a big life change—so big it scares you. Or maybe this is your season of small—allowing a simple shift in perspective to open up a new way of living.

CULTIVATE IT

What season are you in right now? There are no wrong answers. Write down a few thoughts about what you're experiencing, learning, or feeling in your unique season.

Perhaps, like me, your season is preparing you to do something you never thought you'd do: step away from a dream to cultivate a new one. I'm preparing for a season of shifting my time to the hearts in my home.

Since starting this book, and this journey with you, so much has changed in my life. Cultivating what matters, little by little, really does add up. I'm getting ready to step away from leading *Southern Weddings* magazine to step into homeschooling Grace. Both of these are things I never thought would be a part of my path. But this editor-in-chief is trading the sometimes-glamorous for the always-bubbly life with Grace. When I started writing these pages to you months ago, I was terrified of all of this. And now I can't wait to dig in! Each season has prepared me in some way for this very special one ahead.

IMPERFECT SEASONS

Maybe you're in a season of transition, grief, conflict, illness, unanswered prayers, new challenges, or just trying to get by. Maybe you can't imagine how this particular season could be a blessing in disguise. I have a not-so-secret secret to share with you. Do you remember where seeds begin to sprout? In the dirt. We dismiss the dirt and the mess as bad, trying to keep it off our hands and out of our homes. But dirt holds a certain magic, cradling new life. Your past mistakes, your heartache, your circumstances, and the tension you feel right now in your season—every bit of it is part of your growing ground.

I believe this with all of me.

And even if you don't believe it yet, I'll believe it for you. Sometimes my tomatoes need a little extra support to get growing, and I'll happily be that kind of support for you as we continue on this journey together.

To grow what matters in your life, just as you grow flowers in a garden, get your hands dirty, digging in right where you are. Growing what matters takes doing something that is counterintuitive to how we usually operate: embracing tension. We choose to embrace change, imperfect progress, and imperfect circumstances, and we trust that "in all things God works for the good of those who love him" (Rom. 8:28 NIV). Sometimes God is showing us His love more through what feels hard than through what feels easy.

While the rest of the world is tidying up and trying to achieve perfection, you and I will be on a different path. We already are. A much richer, simpler, more rooted path. Cultivating an intentional life means living differently than the rest of the world. Life doesn't begin when our imperfections end. Instead, a cultivated life is made richer because of our flaws and hardships. I've learned far more from my mistakes than any of my successes, and I've gained courage and confidence from seasons of challenge.

If you are in a hard season, remember this:

This is just a season.

God is with you. He will "never leave you nor forsake you" (Heb. 13:5).

Your season will not last forever.

And maybe this season is growing something good in you.

FOR EVERYTHING THERE IS A SEASON

In trying to figure out who I am and what my purpose is on this earth, I've tried lots of different creative pursuits, self-help methods, and organizational systems. I've gone through five major career changes. I grew up singing and dancing and went to college for musical theatre. I got tired of auditioning for my life and became a personal trainer in New York City, where I loved helping people feel alive in their own skin. Hurricane Ivan took me out of the city to help my parents in Florida, where I started a wedding planning company. I met Ari when he was training with the navy and, after eloping in Las Vegas, we moved to Los Angeles, where I did flowers for celebrity weddings. When Ari was deployed to Iraq, I needed a project to keep my mind off of bomb threats. So with no formal training, I started a wedding magazine.

The pits and twists in my story made me feel guilty for not having a more linear path. Why couldn't I just stick with one career? Why did I have to fail so often? Why couldn't I just keep it all together?

Cultivating an intentional life has been a process for me, not an overnight occurrence. I have come to realize that I was created this way on purpose by a good and knowing God, who made me to grow through imperfect progress.

God didn't design us to come out of our mothers' wombs into instant adulthood. He intentionally created us to grow, change, and learn over time, through different seasons—not all at once. The truth is, I'm fearfully, imperfectly, and wonderfully made. And so are you. There have been many times of transformation in my life—not a single, all-at-once event—all leading me closer to the woman God created me to be. Like layers of petals that come undone over time to reveal a fruitful center, I've been in a continual state of coming undone.

It turns out that coming undone is part of coming alive.

When I look back now, I see the purpose in my unconventional path and the seasons I experienced. I see how God used pain to cultivate in me a deeper faith and gratitude. I marvel at how the seemingly unrelated pieces fit together to create a much bigger picture than I could see at the time—and perhaps bigger than I can see now.

- Theatre taught me about how music, sound, lighting, and meaningful words can be used to tell powerful stories.

- Being a personal trainer allowed me to learn about people's struggles and fears, and discover how they can overcome these struggles and fears to ignite change.
- Creating a wedding magazine helped me learn to write words that instill hope in others and gave me the opportunity to use what I had learned in theatre to bring stories to life in the imagery we create and curate.

I'm now a wife and a mother. I have a team of eight women I work alongside from my home office, and *Southern Weddings* magazine is about to turn ten years old. Ari and I recently celebrated ten years together, too, and we know without a doubt that every single bit of our mess has become our message.

CULTIVATE IT

What seasons have you gone through in your life, and what has each season taught you? Write out a few of the most pivotal seasons you've experienced. Look over your list and ask yourself, *What have these seasons taught me? How have these experiences changed and refined me?*

FEELINGS VERSUS FAITH

Whatever season you're in, there's one way to do your season well: embrace it. Now, embracing your season doesn't mean you have to love it; it simply means letting it be. The word *amen* offered at the end of a prayer means "let it be." In whatever season you're in, and when the new one comes, practice saying, *Amen, Lord. Let it be.* Open your heart and your hands to what

He has for you. Your season will not last forever, but it might have something really good for you that you don't want to miss by fighting the season you're in, fighting the changes, or fighting what feels imperfect.

CULTIVATE IT

What feelings have you been fighting in your current season? Perhaps you've been fighting feelings of rejection, brokenness, loneliness, inadequacy, or fear in embracing conflict, tension, or change.

Feelings aren't the enemy, but sometimes they can lead us away from truth. Take your feelings and attach to each of them a life-giving truth. For example:

- I may feel rejected at times, but I know whose I am.
- I may feel broken, but I know I'm whole in Him.
- I may feel like my heart is a mess, but I know God transforms our messes into our message.
- I may feel alone, isolated, and lonely at times, but I know that God never, ever leaves me.

CULTIVATE IT

Fill in the blanks with what you know or what you *want* to know:

I feel _____, but I know/want to know
_____.

I may feel imperfect, but I know God uses imperfect people to do His will. Friend, that gives me such joy. I'm not going to write the perfect words to you in these pages. I just have to share the truth that God has entrusted to me and let Him do the rest.

Pray with me:
Lord, help us to give You our feelings and let You turn them into faith, amen.

Whenever I think about God using things that are imperfect, I think of the peaches on our tree. By all commercial standards, my peaches are unusable. You would wonder what was wrong with your grocer if these were displayed, with their dark spots and sap drippings. Your reaction wouldn't be your fault, though. We are taught to choose produce at the store by appearance first, smell and feel second, taste last. That order is logical, but it's not the way you're going to discover the best fruit you've ever tasted. If you were to ignore the appearance of my Elberta peaches and draw one close to your nose, every fiber of your being would melt as you took a deep, long breath. The aroma is intoxicating. There is something marvelous beneath that seemingly flawed skin.

My peaches remind me that things don't have to be perfect to be beautiful and life giving. Oh, the joys we miss when dismissing what appears imperfect or unfamiliar!

I don't have to be the perfect boss, mom, friend, leader, hostess, writer, wife, daughter, sister, woman—any of it. I don't have to be perfect, because God is. I just have to do my best to follow Him.

Leaning into knowing, instead of letting my feelings inform

my worth in each season, changes things. It helps me embrace where I am and grow where I've been planted.

CULTIVATE IT

In what ways can you embrace an intentional life right in the midst of your current season?

EMBRACE THE TENSION

Too often, we believe the lies that we can't move forward in our current season because we don't know enough, we haven't done enough, or we are too messed up. Does that ring true for you? You are not alone.

It's spring now as I write this chapter to you, and my garden is in a really weird stage. Some things are growing, and some things never sprouted. Some things got way too big, and some things are oddly small. There are many green shoots that I'm not sure if they are weeds or actual plants yet. It's awkward. Messy. Unbalanced.

My life has felt the same lately. Uncertain. Unsettled. Un-figured-out.

I can hear your brain, because I've thought it too: *Messy? Uncertain? Can we please skip right to the good stuff?*

Friend, this *is* the good stuff. Right here in the tension.

I'm growing my garden in the middle of the mess. When we let God's grace lead us, instead of perfection, good things get cultivated, right where we are. Imperfect starts and awkward middles can grow into strong marriages, joyful families, deeper faith, and purpose-filled days.

I've learned a few things about gardening here and there, but I'm still no master gardener. There have been countless times I've forgotten to water or weed, and you know what? Stuff still grows, despite my haphazard efforts! Even with my flaws, I get a harvest.

That's God's grace: even though we aren't perfect, He gives us new life.

> You will be like a well-watered garden,
>   like a spring whose waters never fail.
>
> —ISAIAH 58:11 NIV

Grace isn't something we do; it's something we receive. When I take a leap of faith and step into the dirt with God, right where He has me, I get to see His grace in action over and over as the things that were lifeless are given new, deep roots.

No perfection required.

Cultivators dig into the SEASON they're in.

SEEDS OF GRACE AND TRUTH

It's in the imperfect that good things grow.

A flourishing life is possible, no perfection required.

In the seasons we find balance.

We are fearfully, imperfectly, and wonderfully made. Coming undone is part of coming alive.

Even though we aren't perfect, God gives us
new life. Read Ephesians 2:8–9. What do you
learn in these verses about God's grace?

Your past mistakes, your story, your heartache, your
circumstances, and the tension you feel right now in your
season—every bit of it is part of your growing ground.

GRACE FROM THE GARDEN

Be the Bees

The hum of bees is the voice of the garden.

—ELIZABETH LAWRENCE

One Christmas a giant box arrived in the mail with my mom's handwriting on it. I love my mom's cursive. It's loopy and swirly and comfortingly familiar. I looked forward to her encouraging notes in my lunchbox when I was little. The handwriting on the outside of this box (*Fragile! Live plants!*) was as exciting to me as those lunchbox notes. I knew something good was inside that she had carefully prepared for me to enjoy.

I let Gracie do the honors and peek inside the four-foot-tall box first. "It's a tree, Mommy!" A Meyer lemon tree covered with blooms and fruit nearly burst out of the box as I opened the top flap. Mom had lovingly wrapped its pot in plastic and cushioned the branches with newspaper and paper towels. What a surprising and delightful gift to open!

Mom has sent many trees since: a kumquat, a blood orange, a navel orange, a Cara Cara orange, another Meyer, and a pomegranate. They thrive here in the summer in pots by the garden. But when the weather threatens a freeze, Ari knows what that means at our house: the annual migration of the citrus trees. In the winter months they take up every bit of extra space in our living and dining room. There are so many now that we pass on getting a Christmas tree each year and decorate the orchard instead. I told my mom that, while I love them, I cannot take in any more trees. We are full. No room at the inn.

Citrus trees are easy, though. Water them once a week, keep them by the sunniest windows, and fertilize once per season.

But there's one thing missing for our grove inside in the winter. Tied to the base of that first tree she sent was a golden yellow ribbon and a little booklet my mom had created for us, with hand-drawn illustrations of the trees. Before I could explain the booklet to Gracie, she squealed with delight, "Bees! Bzzzzzzzzz! We get to be the bees!"

Like clockwork, right around Christmas Day each year, the trees begin to bloom. The scent is heavenly—a breath of fresh air in the middle of a usually packed holiday season—and it's our signal to break out the paintbrushes and dust pollen from one flower to the next so that the trees produce fruit.

This year I let Gracie be the bees all by herself. I handed her the paintbrush and watched as she carefully transferred pollen from one flower to the next. She buzzed and hummed, as all good bees do.

Meyer lemons, when grown outdoors for half the year and indoors for the other half, take a full year to produce ripe yellow fruit. But the wait is worth it. They are juicy, sweet lemons— sweet enough to eat by the slice. As we squeeze out every last drop of juice, I reflect on the delight of cultivating these sunny fruits over the course of the year. The annual migration of the trees and Ari's usual grunts of disdain (we pay him back with lemonade), the summers being watered with the hose by Gracie in her bathing suit (no better way to water trees in hot months!), and the winters spent being the bees—the citrus trees are a delight.

Gracie has already made big plans for her lemonade stand this summer. I think she should charge ten dollars a cup. That bee worked hard!

CHAPTER 3

DREAM LIKE A GARDENER

LIE: My life needs to look like EVERYONE ELSE'S.

TRUTH: I have a life to grow that is as UNIQUE as I am.

In the thick of wading through the grief of a miscarriage, Ari and I felt the sting of disappointment over and over. It was heavy. It was real. And it was private. We knew many people who were going through greater struggles than we were, so we kept our feelings close to us.

We didn't know it at the time, but our hearts were being prepared and changed for what was to come.

I sensed that God was telling me to step forward in faith and cultivate something good in the emptiness I felt. So I made a decision to take one small step forward.

I decided to go ahead and plant a garden that year—my second year of gardening.

I knew Grace would love it, and I couldn't stare at the empty garden patch any longer. It seemed like a small step. It was just planting a garden. But it was my decision to move one step forward in faith, trusting that something good would grow out of this season of grief.

> There are two seasonal diversions that can ease the bite of any winter. One is the January thaw. The other is the seed catalogues.
>
> —HAL BORLAND

Grace and I took a bucket of crayons and used the brown paper that had been wrapped around a seed catalog to sketch out possibilities for our spring garden. But it wasn't easy for me. Every mark of waxy pigment was painful at first. They were marks of forward motion, but I didn't *want* to move forward. I didn't want to imagine a spring without that precious life still growing inside me. I wanted to rewind to when our baby was nestled in my belly. I didn't want loss to be my reality.

Sometimes, allowing ourselves to dream about the future is an exercise in faith. It stretches us to let go. We shed layers of grief, fear, insecurity, or doubt in favor of the possibility of hope.

CULTIVATE IT

What emotions do you experience when you allow yourself to dream about the future? Are you anxious? Eager? Reluctant? Excited? Why do you think you feel that way about moving forward into the future? Write out your thoughts.

Dreaming hasn't always been my favorite word or my favorite activity. Uncultivated dreaming often got me into trouble and left me feeling like a failure when my lofty dreams—which all largely centered around me—didn't pan out. But cultivated dreaming is an entirely different practice. Cultivated dreaming isn't about picking a path or goals out of thin air; it's about connecting directly to the Source of life, the Giver of grace, and the One who never fails. This kind of dreaming pushes us to trust in something bigger than we are.

A NEW WAY OF DREAMING

Too often, we unknowingly dream everyone else's dreams. We feel pressured to chase after what's expected, what's comfortable, what appears to be fulfilling to someone else, and what can fit neatly into a box with a bow on top.

But you were not made for a box, my friend.

Instead of trying to make our lives look like everyone else's, let's uncover cultivated dreams— as gardeners do.

Gardeners know that the plants, soil, and weather in every garden are unique, creating a truly distinctive landscape and produce.

Gardeners plan what to grow in their gardens using a combination of logic and whimsy. They intentionally choose the things that they will eat, enjoy, and be able to share with others.

Gardeners evaluate their land, carefully planting just enough of the things that are appropriate for the season they're in.

Gardeners know that good things grow over time, not all at once.

Gardeners use what they have, right where they are.

Gardeners dream using all five senses.

Gardeners look forward to getting out in the dirt, because growing things is fun!

And most of all, gardeners know that they don't have to do any of this perfectly.

CULTIVATE IT

Which of the above descriptions strikes you the most? Circle the description of a gardener's way of dreaming that you most want to incorporate into your own life right now.

Many times, we dream to be lifted out of our current circumstances as a way of escaping reality. But gardeners dream to connect directly to the earth they're standing on, not to escape from it. They start with what they have, right where they are.

You have a unique assignment here on this earth, and your pain, grief, and challenges might be the very things that open your heart to be able to live out that assignment. A seed doesn't burst through the earth and decide to hop to another spot because it looks better, easier, or more comfortable in someone else's garden. It grows right in the dirt where it has been planted.

PAY ATTENTION TO GOD'S VOICE

But how do we know what the cultivated dreams that God has for us are? How can we live intentionally—aiming our decisions and time at the target—if we aren't entirely sure what the target is?

Remember that one of the meanings of cultivate is to prepare land for growth through hard work and attention.

Did you catch that?

To cultivate means to *pay attention* in a culture that feeds us a cacophony of distractions:

Look here!
Buy this!
Take this shortcut!
Do it perfectly!
Be the best!
Do more!
Move quickly!
Listen to me!

It's really hard to hear the truth in all the noise. The dreams God has for us become clear when we tune out the opinions of the world and pay close attention to His voice.

If I set out to grow a beautiful garden using a Pinterest-perfect picture as my target, I would fail before even beginning. If I let twenty people tell me what *they* think I should do, all at the same time, I would freeze up, not knowing who to listen to. And even if I had only one trusted friend guiding me, yet I had music blasting, rocks in the dryer (it happens around here), and earplugs in, I wouldn't be able to hear the voice of my friend.

We do that, don't we?

We try to grow things with unattainable perfection as our goal—and our guide.

We let what everyone else thinks be our compass and measure of success.

And we let the distractions around us blare above the only Voice that guides us to truly live our days well.

CULTIVATE IT

What, if any, influence have the opinions of others had on your dreams and decisions?

If you sense that your current dreams are shaped more by what other people think than by what God wants for your life, take some time to pray and ask God to reveal to you what His unique dreams for you are.

As we try our best to listen to God's voice through His Word and prayer, we are going to mess up, guaranteed. But thankfully, our relationship with Him isn't about our performance.

We don't have to be perfect to have His guidance, and we don't have to be perfectly undistracted to hear from Him either. I often hear from Him right in the middle of the chaos of crying babies and life turned upside-down!

We don't have to fix our lives; we just have to fix our eyes on Him. And not because we have to, but because His grace makes us want to. He will help us.

God is going to lead us, one step at a time. And maybe, just maybe, that mess we're making along the way is no surprise to Him. He knew we would fail and sin and often get distracted. He knew we would need a Savior, and so He sent us one.

Pray with me:
   God, thank You for Your grace. Help us hear Your

voice and follow where You lead us, one step at a time, amen.

GROW WHERE YOU ARE PLANTED

My season of grief turned into a season of growth. I grew a whole lot in our vegetable beds that year, and Ari and I also felt God telling us to grow community. We opened the doors of our home, opened our calendars, and opened our dinner table. That year we led a small group at our church, hosted people for dinner sometimes four nights a week, taught the two-year-olds' class at church on Sundays, and started a Tuesday-night study at our house for couples. But never once were we exhausted from these things. This season was remarkably life giving.

We let ourselves dream about things we hadn't expected to have time for: sharing garden meals with friends on the back porch, picking baskets of produce for neighbors, and connecting with others in deeper ways.

Ari built new raised beds so the garden had more space, and he mixed fresh soil for each one. I filled our new garden space with possibility: twelve types of tomatoes, six varieties of peppers, onions, zucchini, sweet corn, eggplant, carrots, radishes, basil, pineapple sage, stevia, okra, beans, peas, cucumbers, cabbage, kale, sweet potatoes, lots of bee attractors like wildflowers, sunflowers, dwarf zinnias (one of my garden favorites), and more. We planted some wildcards for fun too: a grafted apple tree that produces four varieties in one tree and a "fruit cocktail" tree that has grafted branches of apricot, nectarine, and peach.

Yes, we grew a lot, but this time we had room. Watering, tending, and pruning our little suburban farm helped me grieve. We had made new space so the extra plants would have plenty of room to grow, and I had unexpected open time to care for it all. I had cleared my schedule for a baby. But God had other plans for that time and space in my life. Each day was an adventure in the garden. Grace and I would go out every morning in our pj's and take stock of what new growth had happened while we slept. We'd squeal at new sprouts, dance when we discovered a new bloom, and add a few tomatoes right off the vine to our breakfast. New life was all around us.

And every time I sat in the kitchen with friends, opened our home to host a Bible study, or shared a meal with neighbors, I sat back in awe. The times I got to listen to a friend talk about her own loss, with a deeper compassion and understanding than I had before, I praised Him for the precious life that was lost to our family but still very much alive in our hearts. That little life had an enormous purpose. Despite our great loss, in the garden—and in our home—God was growing hope.

To everything there is a season and a reason—a glorious, beautiful reason that sometimes we cannot see. As waves of grief would continue to come, I would step outside into the zinnias and then smell the tomato leaves. I took deep, undistracted breaths. The garden smelled like a slice of heaven. I was reminded that God is good and continually making all things new, in His time. God used that season to grow our capacity as a family to love and tend.

YOUR UNIQUE ASSIGNMENT

When my Grandpa Cecil and Grandma Celeste ("Bunny," as we called her) lived in Pensacola, Florida, there wasn't enough sunny space in their yard for a garden. Their house was sur-rounded by six Southern oak trees that blocked the sun. But Grandpa Cecil didn't let that stop him from growing his favorite Early Girl tomatoes. You see, cultivators always have their eyes open for unexpected possibilities.

It doesn't matter if your garden is unconventional, as long as you're growing good things.

On his way to work at the furniture store one morning, Grandpa spotted a sunny patch off the highway, under an electri-cal tower. He called up Gulf Power and kindly asked the general manager if he could plant a garden there. I can imagine the sur-prise and delight the gentleman on the other line must have felt at Cecil's unusual request. The man agreed, and Grandpa's highway garden was born.

When my grandparents later moved to Monroeville, Alabama, there was a vacant lot near their house. You can guess what hap-pened next. Grandpa asked the owners if he could farm it, and they agreed too.

This was nothing new to Grandpa. His father was a share-cropper from Alabama. Cecil and his nine siblings worked farm fields that were owned by someone else, in exchange for a portion of the crops.

Gardens can be cultivated under highways and on top of skyscrapers. Seemingly useless areas can be made alive again.

There are countless ways to grow a garden, just as there are many ways to grow an intentional life. There are kitchen gardens, vertical gardens, cottage gardens, raised beds, roof gardens, square foot gardens, window boxes, rose gardens, wildflower gardens, con-tainer gardens, terrariums, herb gardens, water gardens, butterfly gardens—and the list goes on. No two gardens are exactly alike. Imagine your life as a garden. Unique. Purposeful. Unlike any other.

It doesn't matter if your life feels like a vacant lot, a highway plot, or a forgotten patch. God can work in you to cultivate new life.

CULTIVATE IT

Take a moment to consider: What seemingly useless or forgotten places in your life could be cultivated to grow a flourishing garden?

Friend, open your eyes and heart to the unexpected, because our unique paths, in our unique seasons, aren't always going to fit into an expected framework. Your assignment might just be as surprising and unique as Grandpa's highway garden—and just as life giving.

Here are the questions I'm asking myself as I look around at the space and the people in my care:

- What can I do with this little bit of earth I've been given?
- How does God want me to use my unique challenges and experiences that have shaped me to grow something good?
- Where and how can I sow love and grow good fruit?
- How can I cultivate what I've been given—choosing, nourishing, and paying attention to what matters?

CULTIVATE IT

What can you do with the little bit of earth you've been given? Write your answers to the questions above.

Stand on your imperfect piece of land and see the possibilities for connectedness and new life.

IMAGINE YOUR CULTIVATED LIFE

We often don't voice our dreams and goals because we fear that the world's microscope will zoom in on why we can't, shouldn't, and never will. So we hide.

But good goals are about stewarding well what you've been given: your relationships, your money, your possessions, your work, your home, your health, and your time. A little intentional forethought goes a long way! There's no need to hide or hesitate to dig into cultivated goals—no matter how crazy your goals may seem to the world.

I'm not going to hide. The dreams God has for us are too powerful to waste or cover up. As I type these next words, sharing my own personal dreams and fears, I'm feeling a lot of fear. But I'm taking a leap of faith, hoping we can start something powerful together in these pages. Something that changes generations because we aren't afraid to live the unique paths we have been given.

Let's set our feet on this new path together. Envision living a cultivated life and growing what matters, right where you are. What would your cultivated life look and feel like?

I'll go first.

My cultivated life looks like stepping away from a growing business to sow more love into my family. I don't know how that will happen yet. Maybe by the time I finish writing these pages to you, I will have more clarity. It looks like playing outside, saying no to an overcrowded calendar, letting go of the old to make way for the new when inevitable life shifts happen, and letting go of the need to have a plan all the time. It looks like simple faith and letting go of mistakenly thinking of my job titles as my identity in favor of who God says I am.

My cultivated life is a life of intentional listening, something I am able to do because I'm not so rushed—and I'm no longer rushing everyone else. I am able to hear and see more of the blessings right in front of me.

My cultivated life looks like having less stuff so I am able to spend more time with my family instead of tidying the house they live in. I want to sow time and love into people, not purchases.

My cultivated life looks like finding a quiet confidence in motherhood, knowing I'm cultivating what matters in my family's hearts too. Instead of feeling frazzled, I want my life to be fruitful, showing my family love, joy, peace, patience, kindness, goodness, faithfulness, gentleness, and self-control—and His grace when I mess up at all of those things. I want to cultivate a life-giving home and meaningful traditions that help to shape my family spiritually and point to what matters most.

My cultivated life looks like trusting God to work out His plan in His time instead of trying to control things and outcomes because I fear that things will fall apart if I don't.

My cultivated life looks like praying a lot—on my knees, in the kitchen, in my office, in the car, in the shower, and wherever I am. Instead of going to distractions when I feel overwhelmed—or even in times I feel joyful and thankful—I want to stay connected to the source of life and give it all to God.

My cultivated life is not all about me. It's about living for something bigger than I am. It's about living fueled by grace.

Wow, it's freeing to do this with you! As scary as those

thoughts were to tell you, I feel freed in putting them on paper. Fears expressed are brought into the light and exposed for what they are. And dreams become decisions when you cultivate them.

I don't know what the year has ahead, or how my cultivated life vision will grow, but I know God is with me—and He's with you too.

The simple act of writing my honest thoughts helped me to see clearly, and I hope it does for you too. Now it's your turn to let go of your fears and bring your seeds into the light to let them sprout.

CULTIVATE IT

What would a cultivated life look and feel like for you? Be specific with what you write. The more details you add, the more helpful this will be!

Fill in the blank: *My cultivated life looks like* _____

_____.

As you think about your cultivated life vision, here's a little grace and truth: we have permission to change our minds and change course if that's what God says to do. Just because you set a goal at the beginning of the year doesn't mean you have to take that path forever. Who says goals have to be for a year? Your goals may change halfway through the year—or halfway through the month! There are good reasons for that: life circumstances shifting, priorities being refined as you discover what really matters, and so forth. If your dreams or plans change, celebrate! Maybe it means God is growing you. Let's allow ourselves the freedom and permission to change as we listen to God's leading, and let's invite one another to experience that same grace too.

UNCOMMON ACORNS

Imagine yourself one year from today. Picture where you might be, or where you'd like to be. Imagine yourself reflecting back on the year you've just lived.

What would it take for you to look back and know that you lived an intentional life?

CULTIVATE IT

Fill in these blanks:

One year from now, I want to know I _____.
I want to look back and see less _____
and more _____.
I want to have chosen _____
over _____.
I want to have cultivated _____.

Knowing where you want to be one year from now, what do you need to cultivate today? Literally today. However many hours or minutes are left in your day as you read this (even if you are reading this in bed), how can you make one small decision in the right direction?

Your one small step forward could be your acorn.

Acorns are pretty common around my house. We trample them underfoot, dismissing them as squirrel food. But an acorn cultivated can become something mighty. In John's Island, South Carolina, stands the massive Angel Oak tree that is more than five hundred years old, sixty-six feet tall, and twenty-eight feet in circumference. It produces shade that covers 17,200 square feet. From tip to tip, its longest branch distance is 187 feet. And it started with a common acorn.

There is power in a single seed.

A kind word spoken.

A leap of faith taken.

A goal cultivated.

And in the simple yet profound act of taking one step forward.

You have no idea how the seeds you plant today will sprout and grow long after you are gone.

Cultivators think big picture to uncover their UNIQUE path.

SEEDS OF GRACE AND TRUTH

God has given you a unique life to cultivate, unlike any other.

Sometimes, allowing ourselves to dream about the future is an exercise in faith.

It's not about what we do; it's about whose we are. We don't have to fix our lives; we just have to fix our eyes on Him.

Dreams become decisions when you cultivate them.

We have permission to change our minds and
change course if that's what God says to do.

It doesn't matter if your life feels like a vacant lot, a highway
plot, or a forgotten patch. You can cultivate new life.

Good goals are about stewarding well what you've been
given: your relationships, your money, your possessions,
your work, your home, your health, and your time.
A little intentional forethought goes a long way!

Read Psalm 37:3–5. What insights do you gain
from this passage about setting good goals?

GRACE FROM THE GARDEN

All the Plants I've Killed

Gardeners learn by trowel and error.

—GARDENING SAYING

Gardening is a humbling experience. In the name of celebrating imperfection, here are some of the many things that have not survived in my care. This is not a comprehensive list. There are too many to name.

First, let's talk about the year I killed twenty-three tomato plants. Yes, my first problem was having that many (thirty in total) in the first place. I pulled out the dying twenty-three halfway through the season because of disease or plain old wonkiness. For example, my red Roma tomato plants produced white tomatoes! Completely colorless. I don't even know what happened there.

And then there was Big Max. Oh, Big Max. Gracie and I tried growing one of those state-fair-sized giant pumpkins twice, but they never lasted. Most of the seedlings were eaten by our squirrel friends, and despite frequent fertilizer feedings, those that remained shriveled up.

There was the four-in-one apple tree that died after one season. The fruit cocktail tree died too. Apparently the lesson here is that four-in-one trees are no good. Even trees can't multitask.

Pineapple sage is a yearly favorite. Come fall, it is huge, and the bright magenta flowers are a favorite of the bees. But last year I got too excited and planted it before the frost warnings were lifted. It didn't survive my impatience.

I kept my cilantro alive only for about three weeks, enough for one batch of guacamole.

There have been fallen carrots, cucumbers, basil, corn, soybeans, cabbage, and many more. A perfect gardener I am not, but by God's grace, I'm still a gardener.

CHAPTER 4

NOURISH YOUR SOIL

LIE: It's impossible to START FRESH
or MOVE FORWARD.

TRUTH: I can MOVE FORWARD by digging in
and BREAKING up the lies.

Each spring marks the opening of photo shoot season for *Southern Weddings*. Our first shoot of the season several years ago took us a mere mile down the road to a working strawberry farm.

I loaded Grace in the car and drove to the historic home nestled near the fields as the rocks on the dirt road crackled and sputtered under my tires. I parked my car, looked up, and there it was: a field of crimson clover across from the strawberry patch. It was glorious—deep pink and begging for a certain pair of redheads to frolic in it!

I swooped Grace out of the car, and we leaped into the grassy patch next to the clover. As we giggled together at the sight of this marvelous find, I wondered a whole lot of things.

Why did they plant clover in the first place? It sure was beautiful, but why a whole field of it? Maybe they had bees and wanted to make clover honey. Maybe they sold the flowers at the farmers' market. Maybe they just thought clover was pretty.

I didn't know at the time that there was a much more significant reason for its existence. Clover is considered a "cover crop." Planting a cover crop—a nutrient-rich plant that covers your soil for a season—helps to break up hard soil and suppress weeds. Plus, red clover is a powerful source of nitrogen, which is necessary for plants to thrive. Planting a cover crop helps you create fertile soil.

Perhaps the soil of your life needs some nourishment too.

SOIL SUSTAINS THE GROWTH

Cultivators know that plants thrive not because of the type of plant they happen to be but because of the soil in which they are planted. Just about anything will grow in rich soil.

In Chapel Hill, North Carolina, where I live, we have clay soil. So when it rains, things get soggy. Water likes to sit around for a while, like we do in the rockers on the porch. That's why Ari built raised beds for my garden and why I add rocks and shells to the soil mix—to help my veggies drain well.

Soil is what sustains the growth of the plant. It's what holds the roots. The quality and composition of your soil will inform what can grow. But there's no need to strive for perfect soil. Perfect soil doesn't exist. The goal is having *plantable* soil. When you care for the soil, you are caring for the plant.

We often make plans for our lives before nourishing our growing ground first. We look at the surface because we don't want to get our hands dirty or we don't know where to begin. Under the surface, though, in the mess of the dirt, is where new life takes root.

> He who tills his land will have plenty of food,
> But he who follows empty pursuits will have poverty in
> plenty.
>
> —PROVERBS 28:19 NASB

Maybe you are thinking that it's impossible for anything to grow where you are in life right now. The ground seems lifeless and beyond cultivating. I've felt that way too.

REDEEMING THE DIRT

During my hustle-hard days, my soil was depleted. It didn't take much to knock me down. A discouraging e-mail could send my entire day into a tailspin. I had put all my hope in things that easily faltered: what others thought of me, the amount of money in my bank account, and the false idea that reaching my business goals would make me whole. My emotions were in constant flux, depending on the state of the shifting sands.

I had been rooted in fear—fear of what others thought of me, fear of not being enough, fear of failure. Fear ruled every part of my life. When everything began to crumble, God caused me to rework my soil. He poured grace on every bit of my fear and sin, redeeming the dirt and giving me nourished soil in which to grow an intentional life.

Before, when challenges would come, I only had one mode: anxiety. I'd cry, complain, distract myself, escape, or just try harder, thinking I could fix it all. Now I know I have an alternative: trust in Someone bigger than I am. It's hard to choose God's way over my own selfish ways sometimes, but every time I do, my faith grows deeper roots, because I remember these important truths:

- I don't have to strive. Where I can't, God already has.
- I am enough in God alone, not because of what I do for a living or what does or doesn't get crossed off my list each day.
- I don't have to do it all. Done is better than perfect, and good enough is good.
- I don't have to fear what others think of me. I'm following God.

I still forget these truths sometimes, but thankfully God loves me anyway—and He gives me grace to keep going.

Rich soil is transformed soil. Hand over your boulders of stress, worry, and fear, and God will crush them to fine sand with His love and forgiveness. Give Him the thorny remnants and roots of your past, and He will till them up and make them into nutrient-rich growing ground. Lay down your fruitless striving and dry soil, and God will pour out His transforming grace to make you new. Your life may not look like you thought it would, but you'll be so grateful it doesn't!

Redemption is messy, but it's the only way to cultivate what lasts.

I had to let go of the old to make room for the new. I sat in the heartache and, little by little, chose God over my fruitless ways: forgiveness over bitterness, hope over despair, and imperfect over perfect. It didn't happen overnight, but with each step forward, I began to nourish the soil of my life and cultivate hope.

When I was asked to speak at a Christian women's conference a few years ago, a woman I know later told me that she had been surprised to hear my name announced and wondered why they chose me. She knew that in the early days of growing my business, I had struggled in my marriage and my soil was filled with jagged rocks. But what she didn't know, and what I'd never imagined happening, was that same soil being transformed, cultivated, and infused with new life.

Like rich compost, the best soil is filled with transformed remnants of the past. In the same way, your past challenges and mistakes can be transformed by God's grace.

Even when everything on the surface of a garden dies, the soil remains. It changes over time, but the soil is what continues. Things on the surface—such as our circumstances, dreams, and health—change over time and through the seasons, but the soil remains.

CULTIVATE IT

If everything on the surface of your life were to fall apart, what would remain? What is your foundation? Where does your hope come from?

THE FOUR SOILS

In Matthew 13, Jesus told a parable that is perfect for us as we prepare our soil for good things to grow in our lives. He described four different kinds of soil: hard, rocky, thorny, and

He loved *us*. We also felt that God wanted us to love the birth mother just as much as He wanted us to love this child.

We decided to make the trip with completely open hands. We left all the decisions up to Him. We didn't decide on a baby name, prepare a nursery, plan how we would take care of three children, purchase any baby supplies, or set anything in stone. We just obeyed and went.

"LOVE HER ANYWAY"

It's not lost on me that to plant things in the garden, I have to get down on my knees. In the wait of those ten weeks, we prayed hard in hopes that God would grow something good as we stepped forward in fear-filled faith. On our knees, something did grow: our marriage and our trust in God's plan.

As we prepared to fly to another state to meet this baby, entire family in tow, we clung to God and each other. "Let's pray" was the most frequently uttered phrase in our house besides, "Are we crazy?" Late at night in bed, at dinner, in the car, in the middle of cooking dinner, on neighborhood walks, we prayed. We had planted the seeds of adoption, so now we were believing in the garden we couldn't yet see.

On the drive to the airport.

As the plane took off.

When I couldn't help my nervous tears as I got dressed to meet our birth mom the night before her labor was scheduled to be induced.

As Ari and I walked hand in hand into the room to see her.

We prayed. Seeds began to sprout.

good ground. The seed is His Word, which grows and sprouts and produces lasting fruit.

> A sower went out to sow. And as he sowed, some seeds fell along the path, and the birds came and devoured them. Other seeds fell on rocky ground, where they did not have much soil, and immediately they sprang up, since they had no depth of soil, but when the sun rose they were scorched. And since they had no root, they withered away. Other seeds fell among thorns, and the thorns grew up and choked them. Other seeds fell on good soil and produced grain, some a hundredfold, some sixty, some thirty. (vv. 3–8)

The *hard ground* represents someone who hears and knows the right path to follow but chooses not to. She keeps living life her own way. She has it all under control on the surface, but underneath the surface is dry and immovable. The seed of God's Word can't sprout and grow fruit in her hardened heart.

The *rocky ground* depicts someone who has fleeting faith. She talks about wanting to cultivate what matters, but she's more concerned about what others think than actually following God.

The *thorny ground* symbolizes someone whose heart is focused on gaining things here on this earth instead of what lasts forever. She is distracted, perhaps by money, pleasures, or status. Her time and attention are focused away from the Word, and she ends up having no time for it.

The *good ground* is a picture of the one who hears, understands, and does something about what God says in His Word. Her heart is set on what lasts longer than she will. Her life is messy but meaningful. She is imperfect and covered in grace. Her life is faithful and fruitful. She is a cultivator.

CULTIVATE IT

Which soil type describes you? Maybe you feel like a combination of a few of them. Circle or underline the elements in the paragraphs above that describe how you see your soil, and know that Jesus told this parable to give you hope for the change ahead.

My friend Andrea recently shared with me that she felt anxiety about caring for her two young daughters and a new baby boy. Her emotions were batted back and forth during her overcrowded days. "I realized that I have been like the seed planted on rocky soil that springs up fast and quickly withers away. I need deeper soil. I need to trust in God with my entire heart, soul, and mind instead of trying to lean on my own understanding."

I have felt a lot like Andrea. As I grow in my faith and learn to love God and others well, the soil of my life is being tilled again and again. Each time it has been broken into pieces, it has been prepared for new growth. For roots to run deep. For tender shoots to thrive. For our family to flourish.

EVALUATE THE SOIL

Let's dig into your soil and discover what's there, what needs to be tilled up, and what nutrients need to be added. Remember, we're not aiming for perfect; we're aiming for plantable.

As you begin to uncover your answers, practice an essential

cultivating skill: letting the dirt be dirt. Cultivators share their hearts without fixing what feels messy in the same sentence. We tend to do that, don't we? I often do. *Here's what's going on in my heart, but I've already figured out how to fix it. I'm good. I don't need help. I've got it all under control!*

Don't try to clean up the mess right now; just let it be. Get out your honest thoughts, and give others the same gift without trying to fix them either.

You may be tempted to skip this part, thinking it's not going to get you anywhere, but this might be the most pivotal step you take in the process of cultivating an intentional life. In order to grow something new, first evaluate your growing ground.

CULTIVATE IT

Let's look at the big picture. What are you most rooted in? Here are some possibilities. Circle those that describe what your foundation is made of right now:

Fear of the future

Anxiousness or worry

Uneasiness

A sense that there is more to life than this

Expectations from others

Restlessness

Distractions

Grief

Hope

Joy

Peace

Contentment

What did you discover in your soil? Rocks? Thorns? Old roots? Maybe this soil evaluation has shown you that fresh nutrients, or all-new soil, are needed.

If you feel like you just released a dump truck of dirty, messy imperfection, what I'm about to say might surprise you: I am excited for you! The more lifeless soil you have, the more opportunity there is for God to nourish your soil and to grow new things. There is great opportunity right in front of you to turn what feels lifeless into a flourishing garden.

Don't get stuck in the mud. I was there once too. I felt like my mess was so big that it would take decades to dig through it. I was convinced that there was no way anything would change.

But my soil started to transform when I let the dirt be dirt, and I saw it for what it was. I saw the hard parts that needed to be tilled and broken up, and I saw the jagged rocks that needed to be tossed right out of my garden! God's transformation of my heart didn't happen overnight, but little by little, the soil of my life went from nutrient-less to imperfectly full and rich with life. There is hope right around the corner for you too. Dig on, friend.

Pray with me:
God, help us identify and get rid of any jagged rocks, thorns, or old roots in our lives as we surrender to Your nourishing transformation of our hearts, amen.

DEFINE YOUR CHALLENGES

Last winter "Snowmaggedon" descended on us with a vengeance, encasing everything in a thick sheet of ice. A hard freeze can damage plants and diminish populations of pollinators:

bees, butterflies, moths, birds, beetles—anything that carries pollen from one bloom to the next. You need pollinators for plants to make fruit, so what was I to do?

Option one: I could get bees. Yep, mail-order bees. That's something I never thought I would consider. I don't love the idea of beestings or the beekeeper outfit, but I do love my garden. Sometimes we do crazy things for love, right? I did some research and found out I wasn't the only one in need of some bees. Mail-order bees were sold out.

Option two: I could grow lots of pollinator-attracting plants in hopes of attracting a swarm of bees to take up residence nearby. *Ding, ding!* I could do that, no bee suit required. I planted bee balm, salvia, blanket flower, and lavender, and it worked! If you got still and listened to the garden, you could hear the low hum of the worker bees all over the blooms. It made me smile every time.

We looked at the big picture of our soil; now let's get more specific. What froze over in your life in the last year? Remember: let the dirt be dirt. Write how you feel and move forward.

I'll go first. Here are the three challenges I identified from my previous year.

1. **Comparison.** Comparison robbed me of days and hours I could have spent cultivating what matters. It was the number one thing that distracted me from peace and contentment. Comparison keeps us from cultivating the unique lives we've each been given.

2. **Worry.** When I look back, every bit of worry I chose was fruitless. "Who of you by worrying can add a single hour to your life?" (Luke 12:25 NIV). Worrying is like praying for what you don't want. When you look back at the

88

things you worried about this year, did the worry help you, or anyone around you? Me neither.

3. **Procrastination.** I often waited too long to deal with unresolved feelings or hard things. When you realize how broken you've been, and how much grace has been lavished on your imperfections, you start to overflow with a desire to give that same grace to others. Since I have been forgiven of so much junk, how could I with-hold forgiveness from a fellow imperfect sojourner?

Be kind to one another, tenderhearted, forgiving one another, as God in Christ forgave you.

—EPHESIANS 4:32

CULTIVATE IT

What three challenges have you faced lately that have held you back from cultivating an intentional life?

PREPARE YOUR SOIL

Maybe you want to cultivate a healthy lifestyle or break unhealthy addictions. Maybe there's a specific relationship that needs nurturing. Perhaps you long to know that you are living a meaningful life, leaving a legacy, or changing a family tree. Whether it's your kids, your career, your faith, your education, or your finances, if you aren't cultivating it, then something else matters *more* to you.

If it matters to you, you'll cultivate it. But here's the rub: *it has to matter to you*. Real change comes from deep below the surface, where action is first ignited. If what you are longing for really matters to you—if that seed has been planted at your core—then you'll risk stepping into the mess to nurture instead of neglect. You'll stop doing things the way you've always done them and start breaking new ground.

During the uncultivated days of my marriage, if you were to ask me what my priority in life was, I likely would have told you it was healing my relationship with my husband. But based on my actions, my business mattered more. Since everything else felt beyond repair, work is where I placed the majority of my attention—so that's what grew. My work became my worth.

Our actions follow the desires of our hearts. My heart can feel pretty messy some days. I want to do the right thing and make meaningful progress, but I mess up or don't know how to do it. I want to do it all and do it all well, but I'm human. I'm flawed. And I need help.

So how do we grow what matters when we are flawed and forgetful? Jesus tells us the answer: "For where your treasure is, there will your heart be also" (Luke 12:34). We choose God as our treasure, no matter how many times we mess up along the way, and by His grace, the desires of our hearts will transform. By His grace, we don't have to transform our own hearts; we just have to surrender them.

We cultivate what we pay attention to.

We grow what we sow. And we aren't growing this life alone.

> Above all else, guard your heart,
> for everything you do flows from it.
>
> —PROVERBS 4:23 NIV

NEW HABITS VERSUS HEART CHANGE

God could have waved a magic wand to make us believe and know everything about Him instantly, but He didn't. He gave us a big Book, big hearts, and the gift of time. He knows that it takes time to amend the soil, remove the rocks, choose good seeds, break ground, plant, and grow good things.

One year I set out to read the Bible from start to finish. My *why* drove me forward—thinking about the big picture and how I might be changed for the better by knowing God's truth. It was hard work, and I didn't finish in a year, but the time-frame didn't matter. A cultivated life isn't grown from rules or a timetable; it's grown from a relationship with the One who transforms our soil and our souls.

BREAK UP YOUR FALLOW GROUND

The biblical expression "Break up your fallow ground" (Hos. 10:12; Jer. 4:3) means to clear your heart of thorns and weeds to prepare it to be fruitful.

In Bible times, land was allowed to lie fallow—or uncultivated—in order that it might rest, replenish nutrients, and become more fruitful for another season. But when land was in the condition of lying fallow, it soon became overgrown with thorns and weeds. So the cultivator of the soil would be careful to "break up" his fallow ground—clearing the field of weeds before sowing seed in it. When we "break up" our hard ground, the good seed of the Word of God will have room to grow and bear fruit.

Sow for yourselves righteousness;
  reap steadfast love;
  break up your fallow ground,
for it is the time to seek the LORD,
  that he may come and rain righteousness upon you.

—HOSEA 10:12

When I wanted to expand my vegetable garden, I realized that there were a couple of things in my way: two giant hedges with deep roots. I'd go out to the garden to water the plants each morning, and I would dream about what I'd grow where those hedges were: corn, peppers, more zinnias, and sweet potatoes. The space was right by our family room windows, and it would be a great spot to watch the bees and butterflies in the summer. Grace would love harvesting sweet potatoes, and honestly, the hedges were pretty boring. I convinced myself that trying to remove them was worth it and made a plan. I would saw the hedges off at ground level and then dig out the roots with a shovel. It seemed doable.

Well, my little handsaw barely made a dent in the first trunk I attempted to slice, and my shovel hit the roots like hitting bricks. I ended up having to call someone who chained the roots to his ATV and pulled them out. It was quite a scene. A gaping hole in the ground was left where the hedges once resided, open for me to fill it with new soil and some happy sweet potatoes!

The shame, guilt, and challenges of our past can be much like those hedges. They take up space in our lives that could be used for better things, and their roots run deep. We often let them stay where they are because they seem too hard to deal with and nearly impossible to remove.

For me, believing the lie of perfection—that I had to do it all, and do it perfectly—was a hedge that was holding me back from flourishing. This lie was also holding me back from developing true heart-intimacy in my marriage, from leading boldly, and from being fully alive.

So I began to think about the possibilities. What good things could grow if this lie were removed? What new space and energy could I have?

CULTIVATE IT

If you were to remove the barriers that are holding you back from flourishing, what positive possibilities would have room to sprout? List those possibilities.

Some of the barriers in our soil may take much more than an ATV to remove. They may take time, wise counsel, and a slower, more careful removal. Whatever is needed, know that removing the barriers will be worth it, no matter how long it takes or how hard the process is to get there. You are opening up room to flourish. That kind of work is always fruitful.

Remember that in choosing to dig down and examine what soil isn't working, we are going to have to get our hands dirty. It may be challenging and humbling to name our mistakes, our past, and our broken pieces. But, friend, there is such power in exposing what is buried in the dark depths of our souls and bringing it into the light. God can redeem and refresh your soul.

His grace is waiting to grow something new out of what feels messy. You can look at your flaws and fears as impossible roadblocks, or you can see your challenges as opportunities for grace to cover everything. Every little bit of lifeless earth in your heart is a pocket of purpose that God wants to completely transform.

I'm so grateful God isn't done with me yet. Keeping the soil of my life healthy and plantable is a process, not a destination. And it's always worth it. The process of tilling up the soil with Him brings deeper joy with every part of my life that I surrender.

Redeemed dirt is powerful growing ground.

Cultivators nourish their SOIL with TRUTH and let God redeem their dirt.

SEEDS OF GRACE AND TRUTH

Letting God break up the lies, shame, and sin in our lives transforms us from the ground up.

Perfect soil doesn't exist; the goal is *plantable* soil.

Let the dirt be dirt.

Let God redeem your dirt. Read Ephesians 1:7 and the surrounding verses. Where does redemption and new life come from?

Rich soil is transformed soil. It's packed with grace.

GRACE FROM THE GARDEN

Mama Bird Knows Best

The shell must break before the bird can fly.
—ALFRED, LORD TENNYSON

A robin took up residence in our front door wreath. Apparently she had built a cozy little nest in the faux white tulips and laid six Carolina blue eggs in the spring. We were unaware of this, though, until those eggs hatched and a certain Mama Bird got protective. Friends would come over, we'd greet them at the front door, and a feisty red robin would swoop at them and squawk. The next step would resemble a wartime scene as we grabbed our guests by the arms and pulled them into safety to avoid the darting foe.

One time Mama Bird darted right into the house after an unsuspecting guest. Pandemonium ensued as we all ran around the living room trying to figure out what to do. Poor Mama Bird was just doing what her heart was telling her to do: protect her treasure.

After opening every outside door and window in the house and coaxing her with Grace's leftover breakfast waffle on the front steps, Mama Bird eventually escaped our living room. After the robin-in-the-house incident, we carefully relocated her wreath to another area of the front porch. Everyone was happy. Guests could now come over without fear.

Those six little robins grew and grew and now live all over the yard. We've ceased front-door decorating, but I still instinctively duck every time I greet someone.

I learned something from Mama Bird: protect your treasure. Fight for it. No matter how nuts people think you are for flying into uncharted territory, or how hard you have to work, it's worth it.

PART 2

DIG IN

....

CHAPTER 5

PLANT YOUR SEEDS

LIE: I have to know all the details of the path ahead.

TRUTH: Forethought is important, but FAITH is ESSENTIAL.

A ri and I believed that God had a plan for our family's future, and we accepted the reality that maybe having another biological child wasn't it.

We had discussed the topic of adoption for several years, mostly in the context of, "Wow, people who adopt must have a superhuman gene." We were inspired by many adoptive families at church, and we loved hearing their stories. But the conversation turned around, and there we were, two not-so-superhuman people, considering adoption ourselves. It felt scary. Like a why-are-we-talking-about-adoption-because-we-are-not-cut-out-for-this kind of scary.

Our friend Casey, an adoptive mother of six, gave us some

wise advice: "Just take the next step forward. That's it. Just one step forward."

One step forward.

That was doable.

We would see how the next steps unfolded after that.

We started the adoption process with a simple prayer of surrender: *God, this feels crazy, but we are putting it in Your hands. If this is what You want us to do, then please help us.*

We talked about adoption with friends. One conversation led to another. One decision led to another. People would send us links to adoption story videos. People began to pray for us. Before long, the topic of adoption was all around us. We were doing this.

We took the next step and e-mailed an adoption agency.

One step forward at a time, Ari and I filled out mountains of paperwork and prayed through our many fears and feelings of not being equipped for this.

CULTIVATE IT

What is God asking you to step into in order to move forward? Just one step forward could change the course of your life—and the lives of others—forever.

Those single steps forward added up, like individual seeds being buried deep into the soil, gradually transforming and beginning to grow below the surface. We kept moving forward, even in the many times it felt so scary we couldn't sleep. Only God could orchestrate this in the lives of two imperfect people who had never considered adoption before. Yet if God was in this—which we had realized He clearly was—then so were we.

Months of taking the next step forward, and the next, and the next, led me to my kitchen table on the eve of Thanksgiving. The sun had just set, and Grace was happily doing a puzzle next to me as I finished the last document. I signed it ever so slowly, knowing that the next step forward after that was to turn in our paperwork to the adoption agency.

A few states away, my Grandma Bunny lay in a hospital bed, surrounded by my parents, my uncle, and my brother. She had been sick for some time. I knew that night would likely be Bunny's last. In all of this, I felt an all-consuming peace. I felt peace about my grandma's ninety-seven sweet years on this earth. What courage and zest for life she had! I felt grateful for the gift of adoption and peace about not having more biological children.

We had prayed for so long to have another child, and I finally felt like I had an answer.

I surrendered.

I felt grateful.

And then . . . I felt a little off.

I looked at the calendar, I looked at Grace, and I nervously loaded her in the car to go to the grocery store to get a pregnancy test.

I thought for sure there was no way.

But there were two pink lines. I cried in disbelief and said, "Gracie! There is a baby in there! God is crazy!"

Ari arrived home moments later. The conversation went something like this:

Me: So I finished our adoption paperwork.

Ari: Great.
Me: And then this happened.

I showed him the two pink lines.

Ari: Oh. Okay.

We were both in shock, but the most remarkable thing was that this didn't change our conviction about adoption in the least. This turn of events was so surprising and so God. In all we had gone through, He had been preparing us.

Grandma Bunny passed the next morning, on Thanksgiving Day. After my mom told me that Grandma had gone to be with the Lord, I shared with her that I was pregnant and that we also had finished our adoption paperwork. My mom's tears of sorrow turned to joy as we eagerly looked forward to what God was cultivating in our lives.

FAITH IN ACTION

When we told our close friends and family that we were pregnant and that we still felt called to adopt, many people thought we were crazy and cautioned us to reconsider the timing. But Ari and I held fast to an unexplainable, unwavering faith that this was God's plan. This plan didn't have to make sense to anyone else. We just had to have faith in what we couldn't yet see and trust that God was going to take care of us.

Cultivating means coupling faith with action. Out of our gratitude for His grace, we are compelled to do something about it. We often take uncharted paths, letting go, surrendering, trusting, and knowing that we don't have to do the heavy lifting. In a sense, faith in action is a lot like working in the garden. No matter how hard I work in my garden, my efforts alone don't *force* plants to grow. I do my part by carefully planting, watering, fertilizing, and pruning—and then I wait and trust that God will do His part to cause the growth.

There's balance in the garden.

Beautiful, life-giving balance.

Do you know how to grow big, fluffy, beautiful peonies? You dig into the soil, place the bulbs in the ground with some nutrients, and besides watering in the hot months . . . you simply wait.

You take a leap of faith—and you let God do His thing.

You trust that God will provide sun and water and the earthworms to aerate the soil. You trust that when the plant loses its greenery in winter, it's for a reason—to let that energy go somewhere else. The bulb is smart. It knows that it needs to rest and transform and store up energy for spring. And when that bulb finally sprouts again after the frost lifts and the blooms unfurl, you get to enjoy the ruffled petals and marvel at what stepping into the dirt and trusting God can do.

> So neither the one who plants nor the one who waters is anything, but only God, who makes things grow.
>
> —1 CORINTHIANS 3:7 NIV

We can't do it alone, but we have an important role to play. We plant and trust. It's a choice we make—a combination of action (planting) and faith (trusting)—that moves the results out of our hands and into God's.

CULTIVATE IT

Read Psalm 104:14. What do you learn from this verse about God's role in the process of cultivating? What is our role?

My friend Jeane has thirty-six children: five biological and thirty-one adopted. She has her hands full! I asked what her advice is for women who are struggling to "do it all." Her answer: "First define what your 'all' is. Then run from that. God does not call us to that." You do not have to be Superwoman!

You likely have heard the popular phrase: "She believed she could, so she did." Those words are lovely and instill confidence, but that doesn't last. I know a deeper truth: *She believed she couldn't, so He did.*

You don't have to make it all happen. You just have to take one step forward in faith and let Him do the rest.

Where you can't, God already has.

CULTIVATE IT

In which areas of your life are you struggling to let go of control? Fill in the blanks: _____ [your name] *believed she couldn't, but God* _____.

I believed I couldn't possibly have the strength to adopt a baby and simultaneously trust in His plans for the life inside my belly, but God carried me. He carried all of us. This is grace. The great exchange of our weakness for His strength, our unbelief for His very real love, our inadequacy for His power, and our mess for His message.

> But he said to me, "My grace is sufficient for you, for my power is made perfect in weakness." Therefore I will boast all the more gladly of my weaknesses, so that the power of Christ may rest upon me.
>
> −2 CORINTHIANS 12:9

Grace healed my marriage where there was no love remaining.

Grace set me free from shame and striving.

Grace made me a gardener.

Grace carried us when we didn't have the faith or strength to walk on our own.

ABIDE IN THE VINE

In John 15, Jesus used a vivid picture of cultivating a vine to illustrate our need for Him:

> I am the true vine, and my Father is the vinedresser. Every branch in me that does not bear fruit he takes away, and every branch that does bear fruit he prunes, that it may bear more fruit. . . . Abide in me, and I in you. As the branch cannot bear fruit by itself, unless it abides in the vine, neither can you, unless you abide in me. I am the vine; you are the branches. Whoever abides in me and I in him, he it is that bears much fruit, for apart from me you can do nothing. (vv. 1–2, 4–5)

A branch of a vine cannot bear fruit unless it abides in—or is in close connection with—the vine. A branch will thrive only when it is able to receive the nourishment of the vine. Likewise, we cannot bear any real, lasting fruit in our lives unless we also abide in—or maintain a close relationship with—Him.

Friend, this is a powerful truth.

We can't grow anything good without God, and there is freedom in knowing we don't have to grow good things on our own. And there's freedom to take leaps of faith because we know who is lifting us up as we leap!

A FARMER'S FAITH

We live in a suburban neighborhood that is nestled in farm country. There are cows (milk cows and Angus), horses (for riding), miniature donkeys (I'm not entirely sure what they're doing here!), and lots of vegetable farms (corn, okra, tomatoes, soybeans, blueberries, etc.) all around our community, dotting the landscape with life.

When rough weather hits, I often think of our hardworking farmer friends. Growing things is an exercise in optimism. It's expectant hope.

> Faith shows the reality of what we hope for; it is the evidence of things we cannot see.
>
> —HEBREWS 11:1 NLT

Farmers take a leap of faith each growing season, trusting that what they plant will actually grow. They plant seeds in faith and then believe in what they can't yet see. They pray that the weather will be kind, bringing adequate sun and just enough water. They trust in the life inside of the seeds they sow, hoping they will do what they were created to do: grow.

Cultivating an intentional life is also faith in action. It means planting dreams in faith, even when we don't know exactly how those dreams will grow—or if they will grow at all.

But the possibility is worth the planting.

CULTIVATE IT

In which areas of your life, or circumstances, do you need a farmer's faith?

When we plant something, we can't predict exactly how it will grow. When I plant tomatoes in my garden, I trust I'll get tomatoes, but I don't know exactly how many or which direction the vines will grow. I don't know from the start the exact amount of water that will be needed over the entire season to keep them happy until harvest. I don't know what the weather will be like every day. I can't tell you the exact date that the tomatoes will be perfectly ripe or how many I will harvest in total. I just know I'm growing tomatoes. If I pay attention to them along the way, caring for them little by little, then I can trust that my plants will be fruitful.

Many times we want to have the perfect path to the dreams God has given us and to know all the details of how we will achieve those dreams from the start. We want to know the plan. We want to know exactly what it's going to take to grow what we want—whether it's a business, a relationship, an education, a project, or a move. We want details—all of them. Why?

CULTIVATE IT

Why do you crave the certainty of a solid and predictable plan?

God's grace compels us to take our greatest and most powerful leaps of faith—the ones that change everything—even when we can't see the exact outcomes or what we can see feels impossible.

In Joshua 3, we see this come to life. It was harvest season, and the Jordan River was overflowing its banks. Joshua and all of the Israelites needed to cross over. How in the world would this happen? God's instructions for the priests who would lead the way: "When you reach the edge of the Jordan's waters, go and stand in the river." He promised them that the moment they set their feet in the rushing waters, it would dry up. Can you imagine? Hundreds of thousands of people are behind you, and a powerful, rushing river is before you. There is no logical or predictable path forward, and your own strength would surely fail. The only option: a literal step of faith. As soon as the priests set foot in the Jordan, its waters were cut off. All the Israelites crossed safely. His plan may not always be predictable, but it is solid.

Whatever God is asking you to do, you can take that first step of faith . . . and trust Him.

And as you step out in faith and continue along the path of following God, you will inevitably come to a point when you realize that—no matter what path He puts you on—the ultimate reward is a relationship with Him. All the titles, recognition, dollars, and seemingly certain things in the world won't satisfy you apart from Him. They can't satisfy because they are as fleeting as a seedling in 102-degree heat.

The grass withers, the flower fades,
> but the word of our God will stand forever.

—ISAIAH 40:8

We want to know every detail of the plan—and to be assured that the outcome will be positive and in our comfort zones—before we begin something, but here's a question for you: Are you planning an intentional life, or are you planting one?

With no plants yet sprouting, place your foot on the bevel of the shovel. And even if you are afraid and trembling, press in. Take the next step forward in faith, believing in the possibilities ahead. If God plants a dream in your heart, you can trust Him to walk alongside you—cultivating you and causing growth—until the harvest.

Don't know where to start? One of the most powerful action steps we can take as we evaluate our growing ground and get ready to plant new seeds is prayer. Prayer couples action with faith.

If you're like me, someone else suggesting that I pray makes me feel a little hesitant. Prayer is so personal, and it's sometimes scary because it can feel like a giant unknown. How do you pray? How do you know what to say?

Try this. Simply tell God what is on your heart and ask Him to help you. Prayer doesn't have to be complicated.

Just as God designed simple nutrients to grow plants, I think simple prayers can sprout our faith in big ways.

Pray with me:
God, show us the way to cultivate new life with You, amen.

Prayer changes things. Prayer isn't just asking for things; it's an act of surrender. We place our worries, fears, dreams, and questions in God's hands and let go. We cultivate trust in the ultimate Cultivator.

THE SECRET IS HIM

My pregnant belly grew round as we became active in our adoption match process. There were days that fear tried to drown my faith. I sometimes caught myself believing the lie that God isn't faithful. Maybe we would miscarry again. Maybe this adoption wouldn't happen. Maybe this would be the hardest season of our lives. Maybe. How easily I forget what He has already done!

We are all given a choice: believe the lies, or listen to the truth and keep stepping forward in faith—through all our imperfections and times we plain old forget that God is God.

Pray with me:
Lord, may we keep choosing truth over lies and sur-render over trying to be in control. And when we don't, may we remember that Your grace is real. Help us to trust You, and to remember that You are faithful, step by step! Amen.

The secret to having fearless faith in planting seeds, em-bracing the imperfect, and growing what matters is God Himself. Not a new organizational system, a planner, a clean closet, or new storage bins. Staying connected to the Source of life gives us life.

Cultivators have FAITH - believing in what they can't yet see.

SEEDS OF GRACE AND TRUTH

Forethought is important, but faith is essential.

Consider my friend Casey's wise advice: "Just take the next step forward. That's it. Just one step forward."

Instead of the popular phrase "She believed she could, so she did," consider this truth: *She believed she couldn't, so He did.*

Having farmer's faith means cultivating something bigger than we are. We step forward in faith to cultivate the things that really matter, believing in what we can't yet see.

"Faith is confidence in what we hope for and assurance about what we do not see" (Heb. 11:1 NIV).

Are you planting an intentional life or just planning one?

Prayer changes things. Prayer isn't just asking for things; it's an act of surrender. We place our worries, fears, dreams, and questions in God's hands and let go. We cultivate trust in the ultimate Cultivator.

111

GRACE FROM THE GARDEN

U-Pick Memories

An optimistic gardener is one who believes
that whatever goes down must come up.
—LESLIE HALL

July means three things: blueberries, watermelon, and fireworks.

Pyrotechnics are in my mom's blood. I am laughing as I type this, thinking of the dozens of times my mom would scoop up my younger brother and me and drive across state lines for sparklers. It was a life lesson in cultivating joy. She'd do just about anything to grow great memories in our family: cross-country road trips, home-cooked meals, and the occasional trip from Florida to Alabama for some Phantom Cannonballs.

For less flammable fare, in our garden we grow cannonball watermelons, which are a taste explosion.

And each July we pick blueberries right down the street at Wanda's house.

If we ever had to uproot our lives and move, I know I could grow a garden wherever we went. Occasionally I catch myself dreaming about more land, where I would grow an entire field of zinnias for Grace (and me) to play in. But where else would I find U-pick blueberries in walking distance?

Blueberry picking lasts for only a few short weeks, depending on the weather and rain that year. We rise early on Wednesdays and Saturdays, the only two days that Wanda and her husband open their fields to friends and neighbors. You must go early before the summer sun presses too hard—and before the best berry bushes get picked over.

Baskets in hand, we head off to the berry patch as a family tradition. A just-picked blueberry—sweet and warm from the sun—releases a burst of juice and a flood of memories. My mom would take us along dirt roads in rural Alabama to pick wild dewberries, blueberries, and persimmons. My dad once drove us all an hour outside of town to pick the biggest blueberries I'd ever seen. And I remember the first time I brought Grace to Wanda's blueberry patch. Her purple fingertips and lips assured me that this tradition had indeed been passed on to her. More fruit ends up in her mouth than in her basket, but Wanda and her family don't mind. They love her enthusiasm and joy with every berry that bursts in her mouth.

When you pick the fruit yourself, you savor it in a different way than you do regular grocery fare. You're not just savoring the taste; you're savoring memories. You remember the warmth of the berries that soaked in the sun all day and the sound of them dropping in your bucket—*plop, plop*—announcing the sweetness of the hot season. You remember the neighbors you chatted with through the silvery leaves of the blueberry bushes. You remember Wanda getting teary-eyed when you showed up one July with a round belly, and you told her about your adoption too. She was so happy there would, Lord willing, be two more little ones to savor the fruit of her field next season.

Getting berries at the grocery store certainly would be easier and faster, but, oh, how much we would miss if we chose fast over slow and consumption over connecting. Instant food invites fast pace and not much thought. But picking your own sets an entirely different rhythm.

Like my mom, I'd do just about anything to grow and cultivate gratitude and joy in my children's hearts. Our yearly visits to the blueberry patch are planting those very seeds.

....

CHAPTER 6

GROW IN THE WAIT

LIE: Waiting is not good or productive.

TRUTH: Waiting is a time of ripening.

The ladies in my office and their beaus are a lovely bunch. Each summer, Ari breaks out the grill, and we host them for dinner. One memorable gathering brought us out into the garden. This was my second try at growing a special variety of corn that flourishes in small spaces, and it worked! It was ripe and ready for our dinner, so we picked the ears right off the stalk, shucked them in the kitchen, and dropped them into the boiling water. Our corn on the cob was as fresh as it gets.

Shucking corn is simple—you pull back the husk and silk to reveal golden kernels. If you've never done it before, skip the packaged stuff and head to the farmers' market this summer. Mom, Grandma Bunny, and I used to sit on the back deck, snap the ends off mountains of green beans, and shuck corn together. It was a simple activity, but simple things can connect us back to what matters. Back to bits of corn silk covering my bare feet, and Grandma's wise hands peeling husks like she had done it every day of her life. Back to listening to her tell my mom and me about preparing corn with her own mom and grandma. Back to looking in each other's faces instead of at pixels on a screen.

You know the corn is good, and you are with close friends, when you eat every kernel off the cob with no toothpicks in sight. It was a memorable, fresh-from-the-garden meal. I had waited all season for the corn to ripen, and it ripened right on time.

My coworkers and I have spent many years working together in my home office. After all this time, working right in the space where I do life, they know me well. In the summer mornings before work, they often find me pruning tomatoes. They know how much my Grandpa Cecil influenced my faith and love of gardening. They knew it had been a year of big leaps of faith as we moved forward with our adoption process and prepared our hearts and home for, Lord willing, two new babies.

I was eight months pregnant at the time, so my coworkers surprised me with a baby shower at the end of our meal. They also offered their best name guesses for the little one in my belly. Kristin gave her guess last:

Joshua Cecil Isaacson.

I was taken aback. How did she know? We hadn't even told Grace. Ari and I tried to play it off and not look at each other to give it away.

Dinner continued. Kristin was the last to leave. She insisted on helping me do the dishes, which turned into deeper conversation about family and our hearts. Ari couldn't help it: "Kristin. The name—you were right."

We all had tears in our eyes. Because, you see, we had been afraid to get excited. Even though I was nearing my last month of pregnancy, our hearts were still guarded. After losing a baby and going through months of grief and waiting, our hearts had become reserved. We hadn't planned on telling anyone his name until he was born. We chose Joshua because of the biblical Joshua's faith and reliance on God's strength, and Cecil as a middle name after my garden- and God-loving grandfather.

We had kept this baby close to our hearts and the journey between us and God. After grieving a miscarriage, we knew that God could take our son at any moment, if it was His will. So we took it day by day. But somehow, by speaking his name for the first time to someone other than each other, Ari and I felt a deeper faith that we were going to hold our son one day.

GROWTH IN THE WAIT

As Joshua's due date approached shortly after our garden meal, the July heat rose into the triple digits. I couldn't be out in the garden for more than a few minutes to pick something without feeling faint. I surrendered to being an observer rather than a doer. Some mamas crave ice cream or back rubs when they get to thirty-nine weeks; I just wanted someone to come prune my vegetable beds!

It was hard to let go of my daily time tending the garden, but I didn't have a choice. Ari would water in the evenings, and Grace was in charge of picking. Pruning, staking, and weeding, however, were jobs that no one volunteered to do. I feared my lovely garden would soon grow jungle-esque. Well, it did, and it was okay. I let go of trying to make it perfect, and to my surprise and delight, I saw that my garden still flourished. We still had tomatoes—lots of them!

My mom came to stay with us the week of Joshua's due date. I was grateful to spend that time with her, and while we waited, she took over the gardening—and all the gardening angels sang! The garden relished the time with my mom as much as I did. I would sit by the window next to the zinnia patch and savor the sight of my mom tending the tomatoes and zinnias, marigolds and citrus trees. The garden never looked so happy.

Joshua's due date came and went. We waited and waited. After a couple of days we were all restless but trying to enjoy one another's company.

Four days passed. My mom filled her time gardening, and I sat by the window, researched scriptures for the Write the Word journal we were creating for our shop, and marveled with Grace at the butterflies and blooms.

A week passed. Frustration began to set in.

Waiting to go into labor is a unique experience. You can't plan anything or go too far from home. Sometimes there are symptoms that point to a baby coming soon, and sometimes there aren't. Most symptoms, or lack of them, can also make you worry that something is wrong.

Eight days passed. Ten days passed. Eleven. Twelve.

My worry grew. Maybe God brought us this far to take it all away again. Maybe we were stepping into something impossibly hard. Maybe I would never hold either of these babies.

I opened my Bible and searched for comfort, for surety, and for truth. I landed on Psalm 103:

> Let all that I am praise the LORD;
>> with my whole heart, I will praise his holy name.

Let all that I am praise the Lord;
> may I never forget the good things he does for me.
> (Psalm 103:1–2 NLT)

I read Psalm 103 over and over. This psalm begins and ends with the same words: "Let all that I am praise the Lord." I wanted to trust in His goodness and praise Him, no matter what He had ahead. I thought about the times that I had waited on Him before.

In the wait—waiting for my orchid to come back to life, waiting for our marriage to be changed, waiting on God to transform the soil of our souls, and waiting through the grief of loss—I drew closer to Him, and that was His plan. Waiting a couple of weeks for a baby to come was so small in the big picture. But God uses not only big things but seemingly small experiences to remind us of His faithfulness. To remind us to trust in what we can't yet see. I am not in control even one tiny bit, but God is.

God was always there. Even when I couldn't see it or feel it, He was there.

I began to feel an all-consuming peace as I turned my worries over to Him and replaced them with His words.

CULTIVATE IT

Do you feel like you are waiting on something? Maybe you are waiting to find a job that uses your gifts and talents well or waiting for an answer to prayer, such as a way through the pain of loss or infertility, to be healed of sickness, for a relationship to be mended, or learning to flourish in singleness. Describe what feels undone or unanswered in your life.

WAITING IS A GIFT

I have often complained during times of waiting. But I'm learning that we are always "in progress"—always in a state of growth. And growing means waiting.

But times of waiting can feel like a punishment, can't they? We humans are creatures of habit. We thrive on familiarity and certainty. We like predictability and known outcomes. Our brains seek out patterns and habits because they require less brain activity. So the uncertain feels uncomfortable. Waiting in uncertainty feels like a lot of work, because it *is* more work for our brains—and hearts.

It's hard to be patient and trust in the unknown, but you can always trust an unknown future to a known and never-changing God. In the wait we are refined. Changed. Readied for whatever He has ahead for us. Times of waiting are times of ripening.

Can you imagine if you got pregnant and the next day you gave birth? Oh my stars! You wouldn't be ready. No time to prepare. No time to buy diapers, or assemble the crib, or learn about caring for a baby. You would have missed the time of preparation that happens over nine-ish months. In the same way, waiting times can also be times of ripening and preparation in our own lives.

CULTIVATE IT

What do you think God is trying to ripen in you in the wait?

It's not always easy, but praising God in the wait will grow your faith and help you flourish in the in-between.

Pray with me:

God, we praise You for the times of waiting in our lives, knowing You are growing our hearts to be more like Yours. When waiting is hard, help us to see that You are ripening us. Help us to trust that the wait is a gift and we will be better for it, amen.

Joshua did eventually arrive—thirteen days past his due date—right on time, and with a head full of red curls!

SURRENDERED IN THE WAIT

Weeks after Joshua's birth, we got the call that an expectant mother had chosen us to adopt her baby girl. We had only ten weeks before she would be born. It had been many months since Ari and I took that first step to adopt, and suddenly it felt like everything was happening all at once.

We were going to adopt a baby. *Us.* Imperfect us. Transformed us.

We prayerfully said yes to so much unknown:

- How would we feed and care for another baby when we could barely keep up with a newborn and Grace?
- What would it be like to meet the birth mom?
- What if she changed her mind?

We knew only a few things for sure. We knew that saying yes to this unknown was God's plan, and that He would reveal the next steps when the time was right. We knew that He could take this adoption away from us at any moment, too, and that His plan would be good no matter what.

STEPPING INTO GOD'S PLAN

Ari and I packed our suitcases to prepare for the journey. We would either come home with a baby, or if the birth mother changed her mind, we would just come home.

It made no logical sense at all to step into this, at this particular time in our lives. Why say yes to this now? Our parents didn't understand it. Friends thought we were crazy. We had *just* had a baby. We both worked full-time. We both had packed schedules. We were already up all night with Josh. Why in the world would we want to shake things up now? Why not wait awhile until things settled a little?

Because God didn't call us to comfort. He called us to follow Him.

And every time we followed Him before, He grew our faith.

CULTIVATE IT

Have you ever had an experience when God called you to follow Him, even when it wasn't comfortable or didn't make sense? Describe the situation.

We believed this was God's plan for us, but it felt daunting to follow through on what He was asking us to do. We knew it was going to be hard, we knew it would bring us to our knees, and, yes, we were concerned about the potentially life-altering change ahead for our whole family.

We wanted to love another child, but more than anything, we felt compelled to do what God wanted us to do because

The next morning we woke up, knowing the induction had just begun. We raced to the hospital when her labor progressed faster than expected. We ran through the halls of the hospital to make it to the delivery room. We prayed, and the peace in my heart grew like my fragrant jasmine vines.

We turned the corner to hear her first cry. I burst into tears—she was here!

We cautiously walked into the delivery room. I hesitantly stepped up to the bright baby warmer, where she was. *Can I step this close? What if my heart breaks, Lord?* I prayed.

And you know what He said? *Love her anyway. Even if I take her away, Lara, love her right now with all you have.*

I pried my palms open.

Our brave, beautiful, selfless birth mom placed the baby in my arms. I felt awkward and afraid and deeply connected to God in that moment. I couldn't help but wonder how our birth mom might be feeling as I held her little girl. *How do I react here? How do I honor this life, and the woman who gave her life?* I looked up from the new life I was cradling, and she offered a surprising and profound gesture: she smiled. It was the most powerful smile I've ever received. Her smile spoke straight to my soul: *I chose you, Lara. I chose you for her, on purpose.*

The nurse asked me to wheel this tiny little new life to the hospital nursery with Ari. We sat alone with her for the first time and just stared at her in awe. So small. So unaware of all the pain and power of God that led us and her there. We prayed, *Father, help us love her fiercely. Help us to cultivate a love for You in her. Help us to love like You do.*

The next morning I wrote these words to close friends and family:

I've been up since 4 a.m. thinking about a name for her, and the emotions Ari and I are feeling. I have felt . . . I don't have a word for it yet. We came into this with so few expectations, and truly open hands, but we also just experienced welcoming another baby into our lives. It feels different to hold a life born of another mom—one you so deeply love and respect. I am afraid to attach to her and call her my own, because she was given life through this beautiful woman. I feel such a tenderness for her, having just had a baby myself. So many feelings! I am trusting that we will be knit together, Lord willing, over time. Through love in the active verb form. Cultivating love over time, nurturing it, and watering every day. And I'm still fighting so much uncertainty and fear. I'm up every hour nursing Josh. How will I have the strength for this? Lord, how am I supposed to love these three children with one heart and only two hands? And then I get still and remember that we are here to serve, not to be served. And I don't have to rely on my own strength. God led us here to love—active, giving, sacrificial, rooted-over-time love.

And then Ari shared his heart too:

I'm having some anxiety about not living up to a standard. I have this image in my head of what adoptive parents are expected to be like: a couple who has been desperately trying to have a child for a long time and are completely emotionally overwhelmed and solely focused on giving all of their time and energy to love this new child. We have two kids with us whom we love dearly, and it has been hard to imagine our capacity growing overnight. But, maybe, like the process of getting here, it won't be overnight. And maybe that will be even better. I look forward to bringing her home and becoming attached to her while changing her diapers, bathing her, rocking her to sleep, etc. God, You called us to come here, and we are here. Search my heart, and if it is not right in Your eyes, help me to change it. Such a mess of feelings right now!

In it all, we kept coming low to the ground God laid before us, planting seeds of faith, hope, and as much love as we could muster.

As we waited for her entrance into the world, for her birth mom to bless us with her life, and for all the official adoption paperwork to be complete, we prayed.

And God grew us.

Certainty is easier, but it turns out that God leading us into the unknown was the most certain path we could take. We didn't need to know all the details; we just needed Him.

We chose the name Sarah from the biblical Sarah, who waited on God's timing to fulfill His promise to her to have a child. Sarah was ninety years old when her son, Isaac, was born. Sarah's story of waiting and having to put her trust in the Lord is a story I clung to through trying to get pregnant, losing a baby, and then waiting to be matched in our adoption.

Another Sarah, my grandfather's sister, lived in the tiny farm town of Excel, Alabama. She went home to be with the Lord at the age of ninety, when I was in college. The preacher spoke of her love and devotion as a mother, and he also told a story that planted a seed in my heart that continues to grow today. Every year Sarah would faithfully read through the Bible. At the end of the year she would go to her pastor and share how excited she was about what she had learned. She never tired of it—in fact, her joy multiplied each time she read through the Bible. Sis, as we called her, lived in a small white house that was nestled against a cotton field. I imagine her sitting on her front porch in one of the baby-blue rockers, reading her favorite book year after year. Little by little she would read and learn, and little by little her heart would change. Her legacy of faith planted a seed in my heart.

For a middle name, we chose Celeste, after my grandma, who passed the day after we finished our adoption paperwork and also found out about Joshua. Celeste means "heavenly."

Sarah Celeste Isaacson indeed came home with us, in the middle of me writing these pages to you.

I don't know where this particular paragraph finds you. I don't know your heart today or what is weighing on you. What I do know is this: if you are in a season of doubt or fear or worry or feeling lost, lean in. God is growing you, even when you can't see it—and especially when your circumstances don't feel comfortable or familiar.

> Forget the former things;
>> do not dwell on the past.
> See, I am doing a new thing!
>> Now it springs up; do you not perceive it?
> I am making a way in the wilderness
>> and streams in the wasteland.
>
> —ISAIAH 43:18–19 NIV

I have clung to the words of Isaiah 43:18–19 through times of waiting, doubt, and fear, and I have seen them come true over and over again. God is "able to do immeasurably more than all we ask or imagine" (Eph. 3:20 NIV).

Trust and be patient as you wait in the dry times or periods of slow growth. God is always at work. In every season He is at work. He is with you. Waiting on the harvest will be worth it.

In the wait, cultivate.

Cultivators ripen in the WAIT

SEEDS OF GRACE AND TRUTH

Waiting is a time of ripening.

We will always be "in progress"—always in a state of growth.

Growing means waiting. It means embracing imperfect, grace-filled progress and tending to things over time. It means sitting in the tension and waiting for blooms to come.

God doesn't call us to comfort; He calls us to follow Him.

Write out the following sentence on a notecard or piece of paper, and tape it somewhere you will read it often: *I can always trust an unknown future to a known and never-changing God.*

In the wait, cultivate.

GRACE FROM THE GARDEN

Metamorphosis

We delight in the beauty of the butterfly, but rarely admit
the changes it has gone through to achieve that beauty.

—MAYA ANGELOU

Grace: Mommy, are you going to do some writing today?
Me: Yes, sweet pea. Why do you ask?
Grace: Can you write about caterpillars in your book?
Me: *(Trying my hardest not to giggle)* Absolutely! What
     should I write about them?
Grace: Did you know that caterpillars turn into butterflies?
Me: How do they turn into butterflies?
Grace: So if they grow *really* fat they turn into butterflies.
     They go into their cocoon and turn into butterflies. Isn't
     that amazing, Mommy?
Me: Yes! It is!

Grace goes back to coloring. A few moments later . . .

Grace: Can I bring your book for my class? They will love
     the bugs!

Me: Yes, sweet pea. *(Mental note: must include more bugs in this book!)*

Back to coloring again, deep in thought. A few moments after that . . .

Grace: Mom, can you write about the ants in our house?
Me: Ha-ha! No.

When I was a little girl, my brother and I loved hunting for monarch butterflies in my mom's sprawling flower gardens. I was fascinated with them, always secretly hoping one would land on my finger and say hello.

My mom knew I loved these beautiful creatures, so she often took my brother and me to a small bookstore in DC called the Cheshire Cat. I loved its *Alice in Wonderland* namesake, but I was most captivated by what appeared in the front window each spring: caterpillars. Each week we'd return, rushing to the windows to watch the transformation unfold. Bright green caterpillars munched on leaves—lots and lots of leaves—to gather energy for what was ahead. They wove and spun and enveloped themselves in shiny green cocoons.

And then . . . stillness.

It only lasted a week or so, but as a little girl, the stillness felt like years. Would they actually come out? Were they alive in there? What was happening inside those shiny shells? Soon enough, the Cheshire Cat storefronts became crowded with kids, and two little redheads (my brother and me) at the front, trying to get a glimpse of the scene unfolding. Something had indeed happened below the surface, and there was much more to come. A crack appeared. A wing emerged. And another. And, like a new doe shaky on its legs for the first time, the butterflies would awkwardly and expectantly climb out.

What now?

There was no use acting like they were still caterpillars. It was time to embrace where they were now.

It was time to fly.

When the butterflies and moths flock to our garden in the late summer, I'm reminded of this magical metamorphosis. A seemingly mundane caterpillar is transformed into a majestic monarch. But what you may not know is that these creatures aren't just for show: they help plants to be fruitful. Butterflies are given wings to help pollinate plants, carrying pollen from one flower to another—many times over great distances. There is a powerful purpose in their metamorphosis, and it's the same with us. God gives us new life through His transforming grace so that we, too, will spread His good news far and wide, helping good things to grow and become fruitful.

So, there you have it, Gracie. I may have typed these words, but God sure has written some pretty inspiring stories for us through the little creatures that visit our garden. But I cannot think of a God-centered metaphor that has to do with ants in our kitchen. I'll keep thinking on that one.

CHAPTER 7
....

TEND YOUR GARDEN

LIE: Small steps don't make a difference.
TRUTH: Little-by-little PROGRESS adds up.

My friend and coworker Emily Thomas is a rare breed. At the tender age of eight, she began writing out a savings plan from her allowance to purchase a collection of Breyer horses. She also started saving for her wedding her freshman year of college. (Don't worry, she didn't tell anyone.) She opened an IRA the following year.

When I was eight, my thoughts about money centered on how much sour candy I could buy from the minimart down the street that day. Had I had a little of Emily's forethought, my candy money could have grown into something more lasting than a temporary sugar high.

CHOOSING TO CULTIVATE

Imagine there is a hundred-dollar bill tucked between the next two pages. You can keep it today and spend it however you like.

Or . . . wait thirty days, and each day that you wait, that hundred dollars will double. I'll do that math for you. Are you ready for this? At the end of thirty days, you would have over $107 billion.

Which option would you choose?

It seems obvious, right? Of course we would choose to wait and take the larger sum. But how often do we choose instant gratification in our lives over what could grow over time?

Every day.

All day long.

CULTIVATE IT

What instant gratification have you chosen in the past? Examples: social media over digging into challenging tasks, convenience food over healthier options, shopping over cultivating contentment, etc.

Why do we choose instant gratification most of the time? Here are three possible reasons:

1. **The big picture isn't clear.** We don't have a cultivated vision of the big picture and a clear understanding of how our choices today add up to the life we want to grow.

2. **Our soil is in need of nourishment.** We are so depleted, worn-out, overwhelmed, overcommitted, and in need of nourishment that we grab whatever temporary fix we can get that day. Choosing instant seems easier.

3. **We have a fear of success.** We think such things as, *What would happen if I actually lived intentionally most days? What would that call me to do? What would people expect of me? I'm not ready!*

It's okay not to be ready for something you really want to do. In fact, it's normal to feel that way because, perhaps, we *aren't* ready. But flowers don't get planted and then bloom overnight. Thankfully, cultivating a garden takes time, and during that time God can prepare and equip us. When we have a fear of success, we often choose distractions as a delay. But, remember, once it has been planted, a seed doesn't stop its metamorphosis. The seed knows it's meant to sprout into something beautiful and nourishing, and it will be equipped to do just that when the time is right.

MAYBE FAST ISN'T THE GOAL

For many years I prayed that my dad would come to know God. Once, when he was going through a challenging season, I decided to write him letters every week, because he didn't have e-mail. I printed pictures of Grace, wrote encouraging notes, and included inspiring Scripture verses and written prayers. It felt a little risky to do this. Maybe my dad would think my letters were too big of a gesture, or maybe these little letters would be too small to make a difference. But purpose-filled love is risky, isn't it? I kept thinking of the big picture: if I could encourage my dad and share God's love with him, maybe he would want to know God too. I can't take credit for any of this change, but God used my weekly letter writing to open my dad's heart. He started asking Ari and me about our faith and about where our hope came from. That same year, he believed in the gospel—the good news of Jesus' gift of new life through grace—and was baptized at the age of seventy-seven. The little by little matters. It slowly adds up. It could change someone for eternity.

How will nurturing growth and embracing small bits of progress get you anywhere fast?

Maybe fast isn't the goal.

Maybe cultivating an intentional life means aiming for what happens over time—like the richness of relationships—rather than getting to the finish line.

When something matters to you, you don't focus on how slow the journey is to get there; you keep moving forward because the path forward is worth it.

The world says do more, grow fast, be big, use these tricks, analyze, do it like those people, get ahead. But that's not how good things take root.

New homeowners like trees labeled "fast growing" to fill in a space quickly. But fast-growing trees don't have deep enough roots to last through storms and drought. Good things grow and take root, little by little.

Maybe, despite everything everyone tells you, slow is richer than fast.

Maybe a slower pace will help your roots stretch deep and wide.

It's okay to grow slowly.

ALL AT ONCE VERSUS LITTLE BY LITTLE

"I can't, Mommy!"

This is often Grace's reaction to my requests for her to tidy up. She is not being defiant—she genuinely believes that she can't. She looks at the mess of blocks on the floor and feels incapable of cleaning all of it up in one swoop. The truth is that she *is* incapable of doing it all at once.

I help her to think small: "Let's start with just one block. Can you put that one blue block in the basket?" Her eyes light up, and she reaches for the block and puts it in. When she takes it one at a time, the impossible becomes possible. She takes the first small step, and that builds confidence to follow through on the rest. Her "I can't" turns into "I can."

The same goes for you and me.

When I am standing at the starting line of something I want to grow—a goal, a new skill, or a relationship—I struggle in the same way Grace does.

Writing this book felt like an insurmountable task at first. If you are reading this book and have gotten this far, that means *I* got this far. If there are any pages after this one, then imperfect progress adds up. Imperfect progress is still *progress*. Little by little, word by word, I am cultivating these words and growing a book for you.

CULTIVATE IT

Find a small block or a piece of a puzzle—anything that is a piece of something bigger. Keep it where you can see it often as a reminder to lean into the power of little by little.

I used to come to the end of the year and think, *I could have made progress if I would have cultivated what I wanted to grow a little bit at a time.* But I didn't like the idea of it. How would that get me anywhere fast? I wanted to have achieved my goals yesterday, and I would get frustrated when that wouldn't happen. So I'd often give up before even trying.

Can you relate?

CULTIVATE IT

Have you felt frustrated by not making fast progress on something in your life? Describe the situation and how you felt.

I set out to change the way I approached what I wanted to grow, doing the same thing I've learned in gardening: leaning into the power of tending things little by little and paying careful attention to the things I wanted to nourish.

Little by little, we learn to care for what we've been given. According to multiple studies, a majority of lottery winners end up going broke and filing for bankruptcy. They aren't equipped to handle financial gain that fast.

Little by little, home-cooked goodies make their way to our tables. When Grace and I bake, we get out all the ingredients and we make a mess. It's a fun mess, though! One by one, the ingredients go in the bowl. Grace takes the big spoon and stirs them with all her might, and I scoop them onto the baking pan. A pan of muffins is a soggy mess when microwaved, but put it in the oven and it will draw a crowd.

I was reading Exodus a couple weeks ago and was blown away by these verses:

I will not drive them out from before you in one year, lest the land become desolate and the wild beasts multiply against you. Little by little I will drive them out from before you, until you have increased and possess the land. (Exodus 23:29-30)

If God did it quickly, they wouldn't be ready. Instead, He does it little by little so they will be prepared and readied over time! What a powerful story for our lives. Little by little progress adds up and, in the wait, we are ripened and readied.

It is the same with our lives. Trust that what you want to cultivate matters enough to allow it to grow over time as you take small steps forward—and some big leaps along the way too. Your cultivated life matters enough to tend it like a garden and trust that the effort invested over time will add up. But do you know what's hard to do? Remember any of this when life seemingly falls apart.

TENDING IN THE THICK OF IT

I often wished I had a different story to tell you about the days that followed our adoption. I wished it wasn't so messy or raw or vulnerable. I wished I could just skip this part and move to the season where we are now. I wished I could tell you a story that didn't involve my flaws or failures or sin or confusing emotions—many that are still hard to put words to. But this is our story—God's story. Broken, imperfect, and by His grace, beautiful.

The days that followed Sarah's birth were some of the hardest of our lives.

I wondered how I was going to be a mom to two babies. I went into it trusting we would just figure it out with God's help. Besides, it was just motherhood. Billions of people had done this before me. But going from one child to three was unexpectedly rough for us.

It happened so quickly. I was nursing Josh all day and night, and suddenly I had to figure out how to feed Sarah too. I feared that if I didn't give Sarah the exact same love and nourishment I was giving to Josh, I would be a failure, and I would be letting down our birth mom and God. When either of our three little ones needed me, I felt intensely guilty for not giving my attention to the others at the same time. How could I love them all in the ways they needed? I was a year behind in writing these pages to you, and the direction of this book changed as many times as our lives had. My body and my emotions crumbled in this flood of new needs.

We quickly learned why having babies this close in age is unnatural. Emotionally and physically, we became depleted. Ari and I began to experience anxiety and depression. My thoughts became cloudy.

In the haze of those sleepless days, somehow I felt like it was all my fault that Grace was having such a hard time with the transition. She went from being the only child to having a little brother and sister, and two tired parents, all within a six-month period. Her big emotions caused me great anguish, and I feared I had messed her up for life. Since I work from home, this was all happening in my house, where my team works under the same roof. There was no hiding the tantrums and the hard days. My team began to worry too.

I felt like a horrible mother.

A useless leader.

I felt like a burden to everyone. And you know what lie crept into my heart? The lie that my pain wasn't enough. Both Ari and I felt guilty for how hard this felt, knowing so many friends were experiencing significant loss and hardship. I felt guilty for feeling needy in spirit when God had given us so much. I felt anxiety over the house not being clean, fearing that anyone who walked in would know I was falling apart. And I felt shame. I felt shame for my overwhelming emotions and sudden depression. God had so clearly blessed us with these two little lives—how could I feel anything but constant joy and energy? I felt like I should just keep my mouth shut and suffer in silence.

And I was tired.

I felt God telling me to quit.

Step away, Lara.

Be small.

Nurture these children for Me.

Live a quiet life.

Over and over I heard these urgings, and every time I'd ask, *How? What does that look like exactly, God? What do I quit? Do you mean quit my business? How in the world would that work? What about all we're doing to help people? How do I do this?*

I had no answers. Just more questions.

How was I supposed to cultivate what mattered in the middle of this upheaval?

How was I supposed to have the steadfast calm needed to shepherd my children's hearts and love Ari and my community well?

How was I supposed to lead a business and a team of eight when I had been up all night feeding babies? How was I supposed to work on budgets and quarterly taxes when Grace really needed me to help her sort through her feelings, or show her how to draw a pterodactyl, or explain why ladybugs like to live on flowers? How was I supposed to continue pumping eight times a day and nursing every two hours to keep up with two babies?

And I was also writing this book, which I ended up completely starting over in this season, as God started to grow something new in me.

One night I cried to Ari about the tension and unrest I was feeling, and he said something that surprised me. For a long time he had wanted me to let go of work so I wasn't stressed by it. But even though he loves me, he loves God more. And he didn't think this was the right time to quit. He said, "God has given you this work for a reason. I don't think He wants you to waste it."

I took a leap of faith and did the hard thing: I began cultivating. Right where I was. Right in the thick of it. Little by little, in the middle of the night as I nursed, and in the tantrums and the in-between, I tended my feelings and all of my questions through prayer.

In the tension and tears, anxiety and fears, I prayed, *Lord, please give me Your wisdom. Help me know what You want me to do, and give me the strength to do it.*

Times of change can shake our lives up, revealing broken places in our souls we either didn't know were there or had hoped to forget. We keep these places guarded, locked up, and out of sight, hoping no one sees them or asks about them. We do everything we can think of to distract ourselves and others from them, keeping these bits of parched earth tucked away in the dark.

We spend so much energy trying to control our lives—until

one day the gate breaks, and those dark forgotten places come into the light. One morning I began having heart pain. Each time it came on, I bent over, unable to stand up from the tightening in my chest. The weight I was carrying, trying to keep it all together, eventually became too much.

Before a seed can sprout, it first has to break through its outer shell and leave it behind.

It has to embrace change.

I didn't want to change. We had taken so many leaps of faith already. I didn't think I could handle any more change in that season. And I was right. I couldn't handle it. But God could, and He wanted me, once again, to let go.

Transformation is often painful. The refining of our souls is hard, but it's necessary in order to grow. Resisting change is like holding onto your shell when the rest of you is ready to burst forth. What was intended to be a gradual breaking becomes a jarring explosion.

God had been trying to break me. Break my need to keep it all together. Break my compulsion to keep the house clean when life felt messy. Break my people pleasing and the belief that I'm always at fault. Break my plans for His way. Break my identity in the world so I would own my full identity—my true self—in Him. I held tightly to my ways, trying to control everything, and it eventually surfaced as an anxiety attack.

I was afraid when it happened. I was on the back porch with Ari in a rare moment when both babies were sleeping at the same time and Grace was at a friend's house. It was one of the first moments where I had time and space to unravel, and so I did. I couldn't slow my breathing. I couldn't stop crying. My fingers went numb. I laid in his lap, and we prayed, *Lord, we are so weak. We need you.*

And that's when something broke. Here's the part where I have often wished I had a logical story to tell you, one that is practical and easy to grasp onto for your own life. A story that follows what our human minds have the ability to comprehend. But this is God's story. Supernatural. Miraculous. My weakness transformed by His unfathomable grace.

I woke up the next morning and the weight I had been carrying was gone.

I didn't decide to let go. I was loosed.

I didn't think about being behind on my work or what might be waiting unanswered in my inbox. I didn't think about nap schedules or feeding schedules.

I just wanted to be with my people.

Disheveled from another night of little sleep, I took Josh and Sarah in my arms, with Grace by my side, out into the garden. Bare feet on the earth, I took a deep breath. God's grace, continually being poured out on us, was in this place. It was a gift I did not deserve or earn. Not one bit. In my mess, He was there.

I stood in awe. His grace, once again, was growing something new.

I walked around the house that day wondering when this feeling of lightness would again become heavy. But it did not fade. This was the power of God at work. In my weakness, He poured out His grace to bring us into a new season.

THE LITTLE BY LITTLE ADDS UP

I got on my knees the next morning on the dining room floor, prayed my heart out in praise for the heart change I felt, and

God made what had been foggy for so long abundantly clear. Months and months of praying. Months of agonizing. Months of wanting to give up my business completely. I sensed God telling me these words that I immediately wrote down:

Help other people sit in the tension and not feel like they have to give up.

Sometimes, when we feel like we want to quit, it means something *does* need to change. I needed to quit doing my job, and my life, the way I had always done it, holding so tightly to the reins of control. When we leave behind our comfort zones and the safety of the shells we've always known, life-giving change pours in. We weren't made to stay in our shells. We were made to grow—to break through, let go, and press toward the Light.

I embraced a new season of sitting in the tension of motherhood and ministry and leading and listening and business and babies. I couldn't do it all—I simply did what God wanted me to do every day, little by little. I began tending to new seeds, ever so slowly, and ever so passionately.

All those urgings I kept hearing from God?

Step away, Lara.

Be small.

Nurture these children for Me.

Live a quiet life.

Step away from the noise.

Step away from the "shoulds."

Step forward from the old story and into the new.

I embraced being small. Low to the ground with my children. On my knees. Hands in the dirt. Less concerned with how I was going to do it all or love everyone well, and fully focused just doing life.

I embraced a new way of nuturing, because the greatest

contribution I make to the kingdom of God may not be something I do but someone I raise (wisdom from Andy Stanley).
And to do that, I didn't have to be everything for everyone. I
didn't have to be the only one to pour love into my kids; God
had so much more to give them than I ever could.

I embraced living a quiet life, because all the loud out there
isn't going to last.

Good things grew out of hard things. I am overflowing with
gratitude as I type this to you. Not because we are out of that
hard season now, but *for* that hard season.

IMPERFECT, AWKWARD PROGRESS

I didn't have all the answers on how to do motherhood or work
perfectly together, and it turns out I didn't need to. Do you know
how this motherhood/work tension works itself out in my life?

Imperfectly.

Awkwardly.

And yet, intentionally.

We often feel we have to live in extremes. We resist the tension of the in-between. But extremes and absolutes can make us
miss the magic of the middle ground.

You can be a working mom and a great mom. You can be
creative and not have a creative business. You can be a leader
and a humble follower. And there's nothing wrong with a clean
house if your heart is aimed at His life-giving hospitality, and a
messy house doesn't always mean you have a surrendered heart.

Cultivating what matters means relishing what feels undone
and imperfect.

My garden is in an awkward stage, but it's still a garden.

And even when I can't see it or feel it, it's growing. It doesn't have to be in full bloom all the time for it to be meaningful. The tension of the middle ground is the path to blooming.

And tending—whether through prayer or attention or little-by-little steps forward—adds up.

Grace is much more fulfilled now that I have let go of the old and stepped into the new. She's learning to love her messes too.

Maybe you are wrestling with something similar. Let me tell you something I didn't know before sitting in this tension: There is no formula. There is no one "right" way to tend and grow an intentional life.

You simply do what God tells you to do.

And you know what? It may not be what you do for all of your life. Like we talked about in chapter 2, we were created for seasons, and seasons don't last forever for a reason. They prepare us for what's next. Stay open, fellow sojourner. Stay open. I thought for sure God was telling me to close the doors of our company or sell it, and I'm so glad I stayed in the tension. I'm so grateful I didn't give up. Tending through prayer—continually connecting with God for help and wisdom—grew my faith and gave me new clarity.

IF IT MATTERS TO YOU, TEND IT

Maybe it's a friendship, a revived marriage, a closer bond with your kids, or a relationship that needs a fresh start, or a place of fear or control in your heart that's been left uncultivated. Little by little, new fruit can grow. And you don't have to be perfect for that to happen. In my garden, it's okay if I go a couple of days without watering or weeding. But if I were to forget about the garden altogether, I'd have a dried-up jungle on my hands.

Tend to your life in the same way, with little-by-little nurturing. You'll be amazed at what will grow!

To help me stay focused on patient progress, each month I create a tending list of the things I want to nurture, ripen, and grow.

Tending is about continued progress, not perfection. I make a little mark on my tending list—a notch signifying nurturing that happened—each time I make little-by-little progress. At the end of a month or year, I can look back and celebrate visible progress. I can see how the little steps add up.

Any piece of paper will work to write out your tending list. Remember to embrace the imperfect! Don't think twice about the pen you'll use or what your handwriting looks like. Don't waste brain and heart space chasing perfect—just write out your list. If you want a more detailed list to use, you can grab a set of PowerSheets at CultivateWhatMatters.com.

Here's the key to the tending list: it's a clear reminder to nurture your priorities. Because, friend, it's easy to forget what our priorities are sometimes, isn't it?

My tending list in the season after I experienced that heart pain was pretty simple:

- Pray
- Read the Bible

That's it. If I could focus on those two things, I trusted that everything else would fall into place. And it did. What truly mattered got cultivated. There's no room for fluff when you're cultivating what matters, especially in a season of sleepless nights. You dig right into the essentials, and let go of the rest.

CULTIVATE IT

Make your tending list. Write out the things you want to nurture, ripen, and grow in this particular month. What are your priorities and things that will help grow your cultivated life vision from chapter 1?

My tending list today includes making progress on this book, loving the Word, creating more of a life-giving home, transferring some of my work leadership responsibilities to others in order to make room for homeschooling Grace next year, and praying over each of our children. Those are my priorities this month. I keep my tending list out where I can see it all the time so I remember where I'm going.

A tending tip: There are some things that need daily attention, but others that don't have to be tended as often. For instance, I don't need to water the mint plants every day, even in the hottest summer months. Mint grows excessively and abundantly. So I don't need to involve myself with the mint as often as I tend to, for instance, the tomatoes. My daughter Grace feels otherwise, though. If you are wondering what the little bit of green is in her teeth on any given day, it's likely from the spearmint in our front flower beds. If I did water the mint every day, it would probably grow to such extraordinary proportions that I'd spend even more time trimming and pruning it. New gardeners, beware: If you generally like mint, don't plant it. If you love mint, consider it. If you are interested in opening a business selling mint soap, tea, candies, or other products, one plant will be sufficient.

Choose certain days of the week to tend specific things.

Maybe Tuesdays are your days to check in with a certain friend with whom you want to grow closer. Perhaps Friday is the day you tend to your budgeting, like I do. It helps me move into the weekend making better decisions for our spending. Your little steps forward will add up over time, and you won't feel as overwhelmed by the pressure of tending everything all the time.

That's the thing about a tending list—it allows you to see progress. It allows you to celebrate more often because you can see what God is doing in the little-by-little. And remember: growing an intentional life doesn't happen by following a checklist or making perfect progress. It happens by His grace and power. Day by day, decision by decision, step into the dirt with Him, and He will do the rest.

CULTIVATING IS A CHOICE

I know why God had me writing a book called *Cultivate* in this particular season. It's exactly what He has been teaching us to do with Sarah. She's three months old as I type this, and she loves to babble. She has long conversations in coos. Her smile is bigger than Texas. She's happy and sweet and loves her big brother and sister—and they can't get enough of her either.

Our bond with Sarah has grown in a different way than the bond we have with Josh and Grace. It hasn't happened overnight. Our bond with Sarah has grown little by little, through intentional decisions that have added up over time.

Maybe for you it's something else you are waiting to see grow or happen.

- A relationship
- Marriage
- Children
- Finances
- Faith
- A job
- Healing
- Certainty that you are living day-to-day intentionally

Often, there is no guaranteed timetable or overnight results when you are growing truly good things. There are just little-by-little choices that add up over time. And there's grace . . . oceans of grace.

It's in the choosing—in the moving forward in faith, believing in what we can't yet see or feel sometimes—that good things take root.

Friend, our prayers have sprouted. Our family is complete with our little Sarah, and our hearts have all bloomed because of her life.

Trust and be patient as you tend. Remember that in periods of slow growth, God is always at work. In the little by little, He is at work.

> Make me to know your ways, O Lord;
>   teach me your paths.
> Lead me in your truth and teach me,
>   for you are the God of my salvation;
>   for you I wait all the day long.

—PSALM 25:4–5

Cultivators tend to WHAT MATTERS, embracing little-by-little PROGRESS.

SEEDS OF GRACE AND TRUTH

Little-by-little progress adds up.

Good things grow over time. It's okay to grow slowly.

Trust that what you want to cultivate matters enough
to allow it to ripen over time as you take small steps
forward—and some big leaps along the way too.

Tending through prayer helps us grow what matters.

We weren't made to stay in our shells. We were made to
grow—to break through, let go, and press toward the Light.

If it matters to you, tend it.

A tending list is a clear reminder of your priorities
and the areas of your life in which you'd like to
make little-by-little progress over time.

Day by day, decision by decision, step into the
dirt with Him, and He will do the rest.

GRACE FROM THE GARDEN

Celebration!

To plant a garden is to believe in tomorrow.
—AUDREY HEPBURN

Hallmarks of Gracie's Garden are the dozens of marigolds planted everywhere. These bright orange and yellow annual flowers get planted at the base of my tomatoes, fruit trees, and peppers to keep garden parasites away. But I plant marigolds in dozens of other places just for Grace. She plucks the petals off by the handful, gleefully tosses them into the air, and shouts, "Celebration!"

There is no need for a fancy occasion or achievement. Celebration, as we've come to call this joyful occurrence, happens for special moments, and just because life is good. Plus, showering yourself and others with petals is plain old fun!

Was today a good day? Celebration!

Did you remember to brush your teeth? Celebration!

Are you wearing your favorite shirt? Celebration!

And in our garden, sprouting seeds are cause for an extra-special Celebration. For instance, Grace and I grew a bean teepee this year. We took a few bamboo poles, assembled them like the frame of a teepee, and let Alaskan snow peas and Oregon sugar pods climb up them. The end result was fun, but what was more fun was the day we noticed that the first seed had sprouted. We danced around the garden, showering each other with marigold petals, shouting, "It worked! They are alive! Celebration!"

It's a good thing we have wonderful next-door neighbors who enjoy our garden (and our Celebrations) just as much as we do.

If only we celebrated our first steps and little-by-little progress in the same way.

Cultivators celebrate every tiny victory.

We celebrate imperfect progress because it teaches us something more valuable than perfection.

We celebrate starting, and second and third steps too.

We celebrate the in-between, praising the God who makes things grow!

PART 3

SAVOR THE FRUIT

CHAPTER 8

....

HARVEST CONTENTMENT

LIE: I will be CONTENT when I have it all.

TRUTH: I will be CONTENT when I live grateful.

Our washing machine has rinsed many a mud-covered toy, grass-stained picnic blanket, and garden-dirtied shirt. Eventually, the whole front yard will find its way to the washer. Often, Ari and I hear a loud drumming sound coming from the laundry closet. We chuckle because we know exactly what's causing the tumbling ruckus: Grace collects rocks and puts them in her pockets.

Along with her treasured pebbles, Grace usually brings home a handful of her favorite flowers: dandelions. On neighborhood walks, during playtime at preschool, and from the car to any store that happens to have these little yellow flowers in the cracks of the sidewalk, Grace stops to pick and play with them. She lifts them up to my eyes and says, "Look, Mommy!" To most people, dandelions are weeds. To Grace, they are magic.

Stopping to pick them at every turn, though, became burdensome. I would avoid taking dandelion-heavy paths if we were in a hurry to get somewhere. The dandelions seemed to be a defiant and devious lot, making us late and getting in the way of our plans. But as God cultivated my heart, I began to *notice* things.

I began to notice these yellow bits of sunshine on the kitchen counter, by my laptop, and tucked into books. They were everywhere, and it hit me: Grace was expressing her gratitude to me through these little gifts. She was trying to get me to see the beauty and wonder that she was seeing.

I had been putting my schedule over something that God was growing in her heart. It wasn't the fault of these sunny little flowers, and Grace wasn't trying to make us late; my life was overcrowded. God is in the small and unexpected nooks and crannies, if we are willing to unrush our pace to pay attention to what's growing.

Unrushing our lives is a risk, though, isn't it? It means we may have to give up something—or a lot of things—in order to slow down. And often we don't like the idea of slowing down, because it sounds unproductive. But we risk missing something far more valuable than our productivity in keeping at a hurried pace: life. Real life. Meaningful, rich, cultivated life. As we rush to take control, we miss the dandelions—little whispers from God that we are loved and that He is all we need.

MISSING THE FRUIT

During the early weeks of fall, things in the garden ripen fast— and sometimes, many things ripen all at once. If we are too busy to go out in the garden, or if our eyes are buried in our phones, or if we're looking at what grew in someone else's garden, we will miss the fruit.

We will miss the gifts growing right smack in front of our faces.

Here are some thoughts from fellow cultivators:

When we're staring at our phones, we miss looking into the beautiful eyes of those in our real lives, as opposed to our virtual life.

—ROBYN

We miss being in the moment, which causes us to miss feeling certain emotions. If I am at one of my son's recitals, I cry, applaud, and cheer if I am watching him play. If I am photographing and recording his performances, I am focused on capturing his performance. Two completely different experiences.

—KAWANIA

When I'm too focused on comparing my life to another's, I miss out on the unexpected God-moments. This weekend was the perfect example. I didn't have any plans. Instead, I had picnics with neighbors, toasted marshmallows with my friends' kids, savored a long hike, and spent time in the garden. I woke up this morning refreshed, filled with purpose, and ready to take on the week!

—EMILY

When we focus on our phones, we miss teachable moments with our children. I think our children help teach us to slow down to stop and smell the roses, it's just a matter if we are open to listen and be.

—IRENE

When we are distracted, we miss the everyday story we are building together. Every day is a different piece of a whole story of us, and when I'm distracted from that I miss the moments that make up those memories with my family.

—CHELSEA

When I'm rushed I forget to do the things I actually love, the things that fire me up.

—SARAH

We miss the little things that add up to the big things. We miss the very things we *want* to grow.

So we continue to feel unsettled and unsure.

And we want, so much, to feel *sure*.

Loved.

Rested.

Energetic.

Connected.

Grounded.

Known.

Content.

What if we are missing the very source of surety and contentment—God's voice—in all the noise and distractions around us?

When I'm rushed, or distracted, I miss:

- My relationship with Ari
- My children wanting to connect with me
- Opportunities to love and listen to my neighbors
- The gift of the garden—the birds, flowers blooming, warm sun
- All that God has blessed us with

I miss Grace, Josh, and Sarah discovering life. I miss opportunities to shepherd their hearts as they encounter God's creation and new emotions. Like my friend Irene said above, I miss teachable moments.

If you don't intentionally go out to see what's ripe and harvest the fruit, you'll miss it. So let's go search for the fruit right now together. Let's not miss the ripe relationships and blessings right in front of us!

HARVEST WORK

Contentment doesn't come from anything I can buy, acquire, or accomplish. Contentment grows from God Himself. No matter our circumstances, stuff, or status, we have all we need in Him. But how do we live that out? How do we cultivate contentment in our lives?

We harvest it.

Now, let me tell you that I do not always love the word *harvest*. To gardeners and farmers, the harvest is hard work. My sweet potatoes don't land on our plates after growing them; we have to get our hands dirty and dig them out of the ground. We sweat. We muscle into it.

Harvest work is intentional work.

For too many years I grew and grew and grew, and got so tired growing things—projects, business, and trying to be everything for everyone—that I didn't have any time or energy left to actually enjoy what grew. In my garden, I've had years where I planted too much, and my tomatoes shriveled up on the vine before I could get out to pick them. Harvesting means noticing the fruit that God has grown in your life and doing something with it. But if you are rushed, or are constantly distracted by what *isn't* growing, you'll miss it.

CHIEF COMPLAINTS

Here's a question that might throw you for a loop for a moment. Stay with me on this, though. What do you complain about most in life? If a trusted friend, coworker, or your spouse were to mirror back to you the things that you are most bothered by, what would they be?

Here are some of my chief complaints:

- I'm so tired.
- I didn't get x, y, z done.
- I feel out of shape.
- I can't do it all.
- I'm so behind.
- I don't have enough time.

What are your chief complaints? Write out the specific phrases you often find yourself saying. Here are some thoughts from women I know.

CULTIVATE IT

Circle the complaints that stand out to you most, or write your own.

- I can't do enough.
- I'm not thin, smart, beautiful, accomplished enough.

- I don't deserve this.
- I'm not ready.
- I haven't done enough.
- I'm never going to find peace.
- I don't feel capable.
- I don't feel good enough.
- I don't like my work.
- I don't exercise enough.
- I never get enough rest.
- I don't know where to start.
- I feel overwhelmed.
- _____

Okay, now what? How do we overcome these feelings or circumstances and come to a place of gratitude? Well, here's what *not* to do: ignore them. So often we are told not to feel these things at all. I've said the following things myself—and to my children, husband, and friends.

- "Don't feel that way; be grateful for what you have!"
- "You don't really feel that way; you are just tired."
- "That's not true—you're doing great!"

When we say those things, what we are really saying is:

- "You shouldn't feel anything at all."
- "You don't know what you're feeling."
- "Your thoughts aren't valid or true."

All too often, we are encouraged to shove away our complaints, as if we should feel shame about them. But you know what? Ignoring our pain doesn't help us move past it. The Bible says that out of the overflow of the heart, the mouth speaks (Luke 6:45), and a complaining mouth means that our hearts need intentional and tender nurturing.

COMPLAINTS ARE CLUES

To harvest contentment, do something that may seem strange at first: listen to your complaints. Maybe there's some truth to them that could lead you forward and help you uncover the good fruit that's growing.

Maybe you *don't* have enough time for the things that matter to you, and perhaps it's time to press pause. Perhaps you *aren't* getting enough rest and need to examine your nighttime habits. Maybe you need to trade time on the Internet for time outside moving your body so you feel more alive in your own skin—not in someone else's image of what beautiful is. Maybe you feel like a failure in your career path because you're constantly feeding your heart with someone else's social media highlights and inviting unhealthy comparison.

Give your complaints a little breathing room, because they could be revealing something to you. Complaints are clues.

CULTIVATE IT

What do your chief complaints reveal to you?

Maybe, like I had experienced, your chief complaints are keeping you from contentment, making you rush around in a frantic effort to keep up, and leading you down fruitless paths. I don't know about you, but I don't want to miss my life because of the complaints.

- I don't want to complain about having so much to get done and miss Grace extending her arms to bring a bouquet of sunshine to my eyes, telling me in the language of flowers how much she loves me.
- I don't want to say that I have no time, when I do have twenty-four hours in a day. I have a lot of freedom to make different choices.
- I don't want to live in the lies of lack—focusing so much on what I don't have that I miss all that I *do* have.

All the stuff of life is eventually going to fade—our jobs, our cars, our houses, our clothes, our status, our stuff, and our money. My garden will too. But what's going to remain is the eternal impact we had on the people right in front of us. It's not that our work, possessions, and resources don't matter; it means they deeply matter. All of the blessings you have—including some you may not have noticed in the rush of life—were meant to bless others. And if we don't see those blessings, then how can we spread them around like fertilizer, encouraging things to grow?

Let's do the hard work of the harvest together now. This may feel uncomfortable at first. Digging for sweet potatoes in the chill of late November with our hands is not the easiest work. But it's like a treasure hunt. We know the work will be worth it. Let's dig in together and consider something that will be abundantly fruitful. Are you ready?

What if some of our complaints reveal lies we are believing?

- Lies that God is not faithful.
- Lies that God is not in control.
- Lies that *we* are in control.

Complaining clutters our minds, keeping us from noticing God at work and the fruit of the Spirit (Gal. 5:22–23). But gratitude clears our minds and connects our hearts to the source of contentment: God Himself. Remember this:

- Complaining clutters.
- Gratitude clears and connects.

Paul wrote in Philippians 2:14, "Do all things without grumbling or disputing." Grumbling or complaining reveals the places we lack faith, doubt His ability or willingness to provide, and hesitate to rest in His love. Disputing in this verse implies an inward arguing, doubting, or hesitating.

CULTIVATE IT

In what ways, areas of your life, or situations have you found yourself grumbling—lacking faith, feeling doubt, and hesitating to rest in His promises? Describe how you feel.

Complaints can reveal self-reliance instead of God-reliance. We often complain to control, to fix, and to express our distrust and discontent. Complaints can sometimes be our way of saying to God, *I do not believe You are real.*

That right there hits me hard.

But there's hope, and there's grace.

Grace upon grace.

Let your complaints lead you to God and to deeper faith as you let Him transform your heart. Our complaints are places in our gardens that God could transform into beautiful, meaningful, flourishing things. Let your complaints show you places in your heart that need cultivating—producing a harvest of contentment by His grace and power.

"GET AFTER GRATEFUL"

In the hard season following our adoption, as I was wrestling with the tension between motherhood and business and trying to figure out how to thrive in the thick of it, I had a phrase I repeated to myself dozens of times a day: "God is good. All the time."

In those days of anxiety and challenges and sleep deprivation, I sometimes questioned why God had us step into such a trying situation in the first place. I felt a lot of anger toward God, and my feelings would often turn into ungrateful words with Ari and losing my temper with Grace. It was a humbling time. Each time I expressed ingratitude, I regretted it. I felt the sting of sin in those moments. My complaints were not only fruitless but making things worse. I was showing Grace, through my example, not to trust God. And that was it for me. When the veil was lifted off my eyes to see the potential eternal harm my words were causing, I repented.

Repent means to turn away from our fruitless ways and choose God's life-giving ways instead.

Repentance is good stuff.

Even if I couldn't feel it or see it many days, God was still good. I fought the ingratitude and complaining with truth.

And let me tell you, it was a fight. Cultivating gratitude—like harvesting—is hard work. But in the thick of it, when we put praise on our lips, even and especially when we don't feel like it, God changes our hearts.

In the many times I messed up or felt the grumbling starting to surface, I stopped and asked God to help me turn my poisonous words into praise. As my friend Rachel Kincaid says, we have to "get after grateful."

Getting after grateful is choosing the road less traveled—the one that leads to life.

When life feels undone and plans seem unclear, we say, *God, I trust You.*

When we're in the wait, we say, *Your will be done.*

When we feel lost or alone, we say, *God, You are in this place.*

When the world presses in on us, we say, *Lord, You are mighty.*

And when we're feeling weak and defeated, and tempted to offer words of ingratitude for the season we're in, we say, *God, You are good. All the time. You are good.*

I have learned to be content whatever the circumstances. I know what it is to be in need, and I know what it is to have plenty. I have learned the secret of being content in any and every situation, whether well fed or hungry, whether living in plenty or in want. I can do all this through him who gives me strength.

—PHILIPPIANS 4:11-13 NIV

Pray with me:

God, help us to "get after grateful" and learn how to cultivate contentment in our lives, amen.

The words we say are important. Words are seeds. The words we say and let into our hearts will influence our actions, our decisions, and our direction. Getting after grateful gives us a fresh start and new life, and it transforms not only our hearts but all those around us.

Paul told us that we will "shine as lights in the world" when we trade our grumbling for gratitude (Phil. 2:15). Think about when you've watched someone with unwavering faith in times of trial. When you see someone at peace—truly at peace—in challenges, doesn't that make you wonder where her peace is coming from?

GET TO VERSUS HAVE TO

I don't know about you, but I miss the good stuff when I look at my life through the lens of "I have to." Life feels like drudgery. Commitments feel heavy. My days feel tense.

- *I have to work.*
- *I have to feed babies all night.*
- *I have to pay the bills.*
- *I have to take out the trash.*
- *I have to work out.*
- *I have to make dinner.*

What if we flipped this on its head and, instead of "have to," we see that we "get to"? This simple shift in perspective could change your everything.

- *I get to work. I have a job!*

- *I get to feed babies all night. I have healthy babies and food for them.*
- *I get to take out the trash. It doesn't have to live in my backyard. I have a trash can, and our wonderful trash collectors come right to our house in their truck to get it once a week.*
- *I get to work out. I get to move my body today, and enjoy breathing and being alive!*
- *I get to make dinner. We have food, and I have a family to share it with.*

"Get to" leads us to gratitude.

CULTIVATE IT

What about you? Name your have-tos. Then make another list and turn them into get-tos.

IMPERFECT PRAYERS

Each night before dinner, we pray as a family. Now, don't get any perfect pictures in your head. Sometimes Grace is singing or dancing in her chair at the dinner table. Sometimes both babies are crying, and Ari and I can barely hear each other. Sometimes I'm stirring a pot on the stove while we pray so I don't burn dinner. And sometimes we are so tired that we don't feel like it. But no matter what is happening, we do it anyway. We know, after all we've been through together, that prayer changes things.

You may be thinking what I would sometimes think, which goes something like this: *Ugh. Prayer. I don't want to pray. I don't feel like it. I don't know what to say. It feels too hard. I'm too tired. I'm hungry. I don't have time. I'm overwhelmed. Praying is going to make it worse. It's just one more thing to do!*

I understand you've been feeling overwhelmed.

I have too.

You know what?

Look up. Look up from reading this right now and look around you. God is in this place. He's with you, and He's *for* you.

My fellow cultivator, your prayers don't have to be perfect to cultivate an intentional life. Just take one small step forward.

Utter just one word of thanks to God.

Try it.

CULTIVATE IT

Offer one bit of thanks to God. Just one! If this feels like pulling teeth, keep going. There is joy on the other side of your words of thanks.

Many times our family's prayers start with, "God, thank You so much for . . ." and we figure out the rest when we get to the end of "much for . . ." Even if it feels like work to get those first words out—which it often does—gratitude quickly follows. We often end up listing so many things that our food gets cold. (*Lord, thank You so much for microwaves!*) With every word of praise we offer up to God, our gratitude grows. And, best of all, it accumulates over time.

Prayer cultivates gratitude, because it connects us to the Source of true, lasting contentment.

As my family praises God for the little things and the big things, the tension in my shoulders loosens. I often find the corners of my mouth turning up to a smile. I'm so grateful to hold my husband's hand when I am able to pray alongside him. In the middle of the mess, we harvest contentment by expressing our gratitude.

SAVOR THE FRUIT

Maybe once a year, in late November, many of us make a list of what we are grateful for. It feels good when we do it. But then what? The gratitude quickly fades. We write something to the effect of, "I'm grateful for what I have," and then Black Friday comes and we buy all the things. When we simply make a gratitude list, it's like picking a basket of beautiful fruit and then letting the fruit sit in the basket to rot.

I've done it. Lists made. Lists forgotten.

Cultivators take picking and counting the fruit one step further—they do something with it! Cultivators savor it.

Savor means to taste or experience completely. We taste the fruit, share it, make jam out of it, and invite our neighbors and friends over to celebrate life with it. It gets consumed completely—nothing left to waste. Nothing missed.

True savoring is worship.

Savoring the fruit God has grown in our lives is the expression and experience of gratitude.

Savoring brings us to the Source and slows us down.

Savoring gives way to stillness.

I get a little thrill when I step out into the garden and see something ripe and ready to pick. As I pluck tomatoes from the vine, I reflect on the process that led to the fruit: planting the seed, waiting for it to sprout, and watching it awkwardly push through the soil, lose its shell, and grow to become ripe through careful tending and nourishment from the sun and rain.

Sometimes I intentionally savor my food by imagining its origin and its journey to get to me. The apple I ate today started as a seed that a farmer planted in faith. The farmer tended to the tree, patiently helping it grow strong for several years. When the tree produced fruit, someone had to pick it off the tree, carefully box it up, transfer it to a truck, and have the apple stickered and sent all the way to my local market. Then the grocer had to carefully display the apples for me to choose. Wow, I'm so grateful for my apple!

Savoring helps us unrush our lives, and it makes us abundantly grateful.

I hear the "buts" popping up in your mind. I often feel them too. ("But slowing down to pick proverbial flowers feels impossible." "But there's just so much to do." "But where will that get me, anyway?") When we intentionally unrush our pace, no matter the cost, we make margin for the meaningful.

Get inefficient for a while. Remember when we didn't have smartphones? We couldn't check e-mail while in the grocery line, and we survived. Our devices have, in many ways, made us busier. But we don't have to live that way. We can choose to unrush.

Unrush your conversations by savoring the gift of that person's life. Hear not just the person's words but a layer underneath them. Hear people's hearts. Reply not just to their words but to what they are telling you with their eyes.

Unrush your Bible reading by savoring God's life-giving Word. Let the seeds sink in and take root in your soul. Let the words swirl around in your mind, or read them aloud and let them find life in your voice. Savor them.

Unrush your schedule by savoring what matters and looking at the big picture. Maybe the things you think you need to get done aren't all essential to what matters in the big picture. Maybe there are some things that could go so you have margin for unexpected blooms in unexpected places.

Unrush your everything by savoring who God is and who He says you are: loved, enough, and fully taken care of.

> Put on then, as God's chosen ones, holy and beloved, compassionate hearts, kindness, humility, meekness, and patience, bearing with one another and, if one has a complaint against another, forgiving each other; as the Lord has forgiven you, so you also must forgive. And above all these put on love, which binds everything together in perfect harmony. And let the peace of Christ rule in your hearts, to which indeed you were called in one body. And be thankful. Let the word of Christ dwell in you richly, teaching and admonishing one another in all wisdom, singing psalms and hymns and spiritual songs, with thankfulness in your hearts to God. And whatever you do, in word or deed, do everything in the name of the Lord Jesus, giving thanks to God the Father through him.
>
> —COLOSSIANS 3:12-17

COMING UNDONE

I woke up a few weeks ago and felt tired of fixing my hair. Always putting it up or straightening it. Hiding my curls. Hiding my discontent. I had been teased in middle school for my frizzy red hair, and ever since I felt flawed. I did whatever I could to hide it.

But that morning I suddenly felt frustrated by this.

So I washed it and let my curls go wild that day.

Grace played with my hair that night, wrapping my curls around her fingers, putting bows in my locks, and simply wanting to touch my hair. Something clicked. The next morning I let it go again. And again. Each day I felt more free. It wasn't about a hairstyle; it was about letting go of what years of feeling rejected had done to me. It was about finally expressing gratitude for the way God created me. If I wanted Grace to live loved, I was going to have to show her how and live it myself. I had to come undone.

CULTIVATORS PAY ATTENTION

Being a cultivator means being a present observer—paying attention so you can harvest what's ripe and right in front of you.

Cultivators see magic in what seems everyday and insignificant to the rushed soul.

Cultivators see the positive potential in complaints, because we see that our words come from hearts that can be changed through the power of His grace—nurtured instead of neglected, loved instead of left, seen instead of ignored.

You may think there's nothing good around you to be grateful for, but look a level deeper. An abandoned, empty field becomes something marvelous when you notice it's dotted in humble dandelions.

One of the most life-changing gifts the garden has given me is the renewal of my five senses.

I see the miracles of new life all around me.

I inhale the roses.

I hear the buzz of bees and the rustling of trees over the rush of the world.

I am unafraid to grab a handful of dirt and feel the earth beneath my bare feet.

I taste and see that the Lord is good.

Rejoice always, pray without ceasing, give thanks in all circumstances; for this is the will of God in Christ Jesus for you.

–1 THESSALONIANS 5:16–18

Cultivators intentionally savor the fruit.

SEEDS OF GRACE AND TRUTH

We will be content when we live grateful.

We risk missing something far more valuable than our productivity in keeping at a hurried pace: life. Real life. Meaningful, rich, cultivated life.

Contentment doesn't come from anything I can buy, acquire, or accomplish. Contentment grows from God Himself. We are loved, and He is all we need.

Complaints are clues. Complaints can reveal self-reliance instead of God-reliance.

Let your complaints show you places in your heart that need cultivating—producing a harvest of contentment by His grace and power. Read James 1:5.

Turn your have-tos into get-tos.

Savoring is an act of worship, leading us to the Source of where all good things originate—God Himself.

An abandoned, empty field becomes something marvelous when you notice it's dotted in humble dandelions.

GRACE FROM THE GARDEN

Heirloom Plants

A man doesn't plant a tree for himself.
He plants it for posterity.
—ALEXANDER SMITH

Many of the plants in my garden have a story that precedes me.

My great-grandmother Irene grew jonquils—a small daffodil with an intoxicating fragrance—by the steps of her home in Montevallo, Alabama.

Irene's youngest daughter out of eleven children, Celeste, must have loved these special blooms. Perhaps they were gathered in jars on the family table. Maybe they were part of make-believe tea parties on the front steps with her sisters. Or perhaps they simply reminded her of their little white house with the wraparound porch where so many memories were cultivated. Whatever the reason, these flowers were clearly loved. Celeste stood on the front steps of that same house many years later on her wedding day to Cecil, and she kindly requested one gift from her mother before they left: a few of the jonquil bulbs to plant in her own garden with her husband.

Celeste and Cecil settled in Pensacola, Florida, where my mom was born. When they later moved to Irvine, California, the jonquils were carefully dug up out of the ground and brought with them. And when Celeste's mother and father passed and the family home went up for sale, several of the siblings traveled back to Montevallo to bid their childhood home farewell—trowels in hand.

One of those siblings, Marguerite, sent a box of carefully wrapped bulbs to my mom. You would have thought she had opened a box of gold coins, she was so delighted!

I have always loved the smell of narcissus, daffodils, hyacinth, and especially Irene's jonquils that my mom grew in pots all over our house in the winter months. The perfume of spring in the chill of the winter is soul renewing, and thinking of the three generations through which those bulbs had been cultivated made them all the more meaningful.

When Celeste went to be with the Lord on Thanksgiving morning (the day after we finished our adoption paperwork and found out about Josh), my mom had the terribly hard task of flying to California to clear out her house. She grieved as each layer of furniture, clothing, and family mementos was sorted—some sold and some packed to come back with her to Florida. It was a heart-wrenching week for my mom. I called her often to see how she was feeling. We all missed Grandma Bunny.

On the last day of clearing out the house, my mom looked around to be sure there was nothing left behind. She walked outside to the garden that Cecil and Celeste had so lovingly kept, and she remembered: the jonquils.

It was winter at the time, so the bulbs were dormant in the

soil. How would she find them? She recalled a memory of my brother and me playing catch with Cecil in the backyard while Celeste made tea. Out between two of Celeste's favorite rose bushes, near where we were playing, she remembered a sea of yellow and white blooms—the jonquils!

My mom went over to the spot, knelt down, and dug her bare hands into the earth. Sure enough, right below the surface of the soil, there they were. After a hard week of letting go, it was as if God was saying to my mom, *I see you, I love you, and I am here with you. There is new life below the surface in what feels bleak.*

She packed up those bulbs in some of the many sheets of tissue paper Celeste had saved (along with wrapping paper from every gift she'd ever been given—a true child of the Depression) and sent them to the redheaded gardener who is typing this story to you.

Gardening can extend memories and keep stories blooming. While it likely never crossed Irene's mind that these spring beauties would weave themselves into the legacy of our family, they did just that. Some people have jewels as family heirlooms; we have jonquils.

CHAPTER 9

....

FLOURISH WITH OTHERS

LIE: I can do life by MYSELF.

TRUTH: I need MEANINGFUL relationships.

I hope you get to meet Walter one day. His Carolina accent is as thick as molasses and just as sweet. Walter is our mailman—our Southern Santa, as we like to call him. When we moved to our house five years ago, I was pregnant with Grace. He brought the mail to our door every day because he didn't want me walking to the mailbox in the sweltering heat. He didn't have to do that, but that's who Walter is. I often greeted him at the door to offer my thanks and chat.

While driving home from the grocery store one afternoon, I spotted a man who looked like Walter out among the black Angus cows on the way to our house. *What on earth is our mailman doing in the cow pasture? Maybe he knows the people who own the farm.* I couldn't wait for the mail to come the next day so I could investigate.

"Oh, yes! My wife's family has owned that land for sixty years," Walter told me with a big smile. "I worked on my dad's farm when I was young, and I've been raising Angus ever since. I used to have a whole lot of them, but delivering the mail keeps me busy. Now I just have the four cows." I couldn't believe it—Walter, our mailman, was also a cow farmer!

Grace was equally delighted at this fact, and thus began her love for the daily mail delivery. When she hears his truck coming, she drops whatever she is doing, grabs her little mailbag that Aunt Jessie got her, and sprints out to yell, "Hi, Walter! Did you bring me anything?" Even junk mail and coupons get her excited, so Walter always has something for Grace. "How are the cows doing?" is her next question. He tells her all about their adventures: getting groomed, grazing on fresh grass, and the occasional new calf arrival. I smile at Walter as Grace makes her daily inquiries, and he smiles back. All three of our hearts are grateful for these simple, daily interactions.

After Gracie fills her mailbag, Walter and I catch up. Sometimes it's cow talk, but many times we chat about a neighbor he delivered to who is sick and needs encouragement, how our kids are doing, what he's "putting up" from his garden (mustard greens this year because his wife loves them), and how good God is. I brought Joshua out to see him yesterday, and the little guy had the biggest grin on his face. One day soon, there will be three little ones dashing for the mail truck each afternoon—the thought makes me giddy.

I would need strong convincing if we ever considered moving, or Walter would have to change mail routes! Our pleasant chats and Grace's joy when we hear his truck coming around the bend are some of my favorite things about living here. We have cultivated a meaningful friendship.

It didn't take much. He decided to be kind to a pregnant stranger, and I simply opened my front door to say hello and acknowledge his kindness. After only a couple of mail-time hellos, a friendship began to sprout.

Whether it's with your mail carrier, a neighbor, a mentor, a friend, or a spouse, you can cultivate fruitful relationships with careful tending, nurturing, and learning to embrace awkward.

WHY TAKE THE RISK?

Many times we aren't fully convinced that we actually need other people in order to live an intentional life. We may feel that it's easier not to let others in. Why put ourselves out there, risking hurt or rejection, if we can do life alone in our safe little bubbles?

We need other people who can teach us from their own experiences, encourage us when we get frustrated, and help us fix problems. Seasoned gardeners can help us cultivate well.

Several years ago, my friend Marcia helped me through some growing pains in our marriage. I took a leap of faith and invited her over one day to get some advice. Soon after, she gave me a box of thirty cards on which she'd written prayers for my marriage, parenting, and writing these words to you—one to open each day for a month. It must have taken her two hours to write these cards. But, knowing Marcia's heart, she wasn't burdened by the time it took to write them; she looked at the big picture—the fruitful harvest they could produce in my life and in my family.

That's why we take the risk: because stepping outside of our comfort zones to build meaningful connections could change not only our lives but other people's lives too. Fruitful relationships aren't about us; they are about something bigger than we are. The fruit of community is God Himself.

> Whoever refreshes others will be refreshed.
> —PROVERBS 11:25 NIV

I confess that I had a hard time being vulnerable with Marcia at first. I didn't want to tell anyone how I was feeling, because my prideful heart believed that no one could fix my struggles. Well, I was right—no one else but God truly fixed them, but He used friends like Marcia to change me and help me see a better path forward than I could have seen on my own. I was afraid to let her in and risk feeling uncomfortable in getting advice from someone else. I was fearful of someone else seeing my mess. But I'm so glad I got over myself and asked her to come to my house for a cup of tea one day. That couch date was a seed planted—a seed that took root and helped grow our marriage.

A garden surrounded by barbed wire that keeps out everyone and everything will soon be sapped of life. Yes, our gardens need to be protected from harmful intruders, but we also need worms to till the soil, bees to pollinate our plants, and birds to spread seeds.

Boundaries are good, but make sure they are also clear and purposeful, allowing for relationships and good growth.

FRUITFUL FRIENDSHIP

For years, I would tell Ari that I didn't have close friends because I couldn't find anyone who understood me. I didn't have local friends who owned their own businesses and were also moms. I hesitated to tell people about my business struggles for fear that they wouldn't get it or that I would make them feel alienated. I felt isolated and alone.

Believing the lie that I had to have friends who were exactly like me caused me not to make any connections at all.

Plus, I spent far too long believing that I wasn't good at friendship. I felt too flawed—too controlling, too emotional, and too forgetful to have deep friendships. But I realized that I was expecting "perfect" in friendships—expecting overnight connections and believing that I had to have it all together to have meaningful relationships. I still struggle when friends do nice things for me, because I feel flawed and therefore undeserving. The lies of perfection try to hold me back from making any connections at all.

CULTIVATE IT

Do you feel as if you aren't good at friendship? If so, why? How could letting go of a standard of perfection help give you freedom to pursue authentic friendships?

But I don't have to hold myself—or others—to a standard of perfection; I just have to do my best to love others well through all my flaws and mess.

Our flaws are the very things that deeply connect us to each other. And it's His grace in our flaws that makes our friendships fruitful.

- Fruitful friendship is patient, imperfect, forgiving, humble, encouraging, truthful, trusting, and grace-filled.

- Fruitful friendship asks a second question.
- Fruitful friendship stays.

CULTIVATE IT

Which of the above descriptions of *fruitful friendship* appeals most to you?

EMBRACE AWKWARD

I thought it was too late in my life to make close friends. I had so much fear about starting fresh, getting out there, and embracing "awkward." What would I say? Where would I look for good friends? How do I learn to be a good friend myself when I feel so flawed?

Maybe you want close friendships, but . . .

- You don't know where to start.
- You've tried and you're just not good at it.
- You've been hurt by friends in the past.
- You don't know where to find friends you really connect with.
- You don't know what to say when you feel awkward.
- You're afraid of not being perfect, of not being fun enough, of being too introverted, awkward in conversation, too broken, and too busy for friends.

Do any of these ring true for you? If so, you are not alone. Here are some of the fears expressed by many women I know:

- "I'm scared that sharing my burdens will make people run for the hills and that I may come off as too intense."
- "I don't know how to start friendships. I fear the other person won't want to be friends with me."
- "My biggest fear about friendship is rejection. The early stages of friendship feel oddly like dating, and if a new friend reschedules or says no to an invitation, I struggle not to take it personally."
- "I have a fear of not being thoughtful enough, not being fun enough, or not having enough time to spend with my friends."
- "I fear that it's too late to cultivate real, lasting friendships."

CULTIVATE IT

Which of the above expressed fears about friendship resonates with you? Put a star beside the one(s) you can relate to.

Fruitful friendships grow not because we don't experience fear, but because breaking ground on meaningful relationships becomes more important than our fear. Taking big leaps of faith, embracing the awkward (lots of awkward!), and putting myself out there to do life with others has changed our family.

After our miscarriage, when Ari and I entered a new and unexpected season of growing in community, God was working out a plan that we couldn't see at the time. He knew we would need deep friendships in the hard season following our adoption. He knew we would need support, and people to constantly remind us to ask for help, and accept it. He grew a community around us.

Where do you begin? It might be a challenge at first, but getting out there to make new friends is worth it. We were meant to do life together. We were created for community. There is a new friend out there who needs you just as much as you need her. So let's get to it and get out there—together!

Jesus showed us through His example how important one-on-one relationships were to Him. Though He often spoke to crowds, His focus was on one-on-one relationships. He didn't have a megaphone or an Instagram account. He had two feet and one goal. Little by little, person by person, He changed history.

BUT I'M TOO FLAWED

I have often feared that I've had too much mess in my life for others to be able to handle or understand.

But, many times, out of our greatest pain comes true connection.

Out of experiencing the dark years of our marriage and the redemption that followed, God has allowed me to encourage other women who are experiencing similar struggles, helping them to have hope. Out of grieving a miscarriage came a new compassion for women who had experienced loss. Conversations were born out of these challenges that turned into connections. Fruitful friendships sprouted.

Kate heard me talk about the struggles Ari and I had early in our married life, and she asked if I would meet her one afternoon to offer her advice. After I shared a little of my journey and she shared hers, we both knew that God had a plan for our experiences to converge. He used our shared struggles to connect us. That conversation turned into an invitation for her to come over to my house. We sat on the couch and talked about marriage, motherhood, and faith. And then I awkwardly asked if I could pray for us. We grabbed hands, and among many things I said to God in that imperfect prayer, I asked Him to grow our friendship. Friends who pray together stay bonded together by far more than shared hobbies or interests. Many couch dates, BBQs, park playdates, and midday I'm-having-a-hard-mama-day texts later, we see the fruit that God grew from that first prayer. Our friendship is growing. Kate's marriage is thriving. I can't take a single bit of credit for helping to redirect the course of her life, but I know that God used my mess and transformation as a seed of hope for her.

God has the same plan for the broken places in your life too. He wants to take them and do something glorious with them, turning them into seeds of hope to plant in gardens all over the world.

First step: meet and make a connection.

Here are some practical ways you can begin to cultivate friendships and community in your life:

- Invite her—be the invitation instead of waiting for one.
- Send an e-mail.
- Offer to help.
- Introduce yourself on a neighborhood walk.
- Talk about a similar or shared interest.
- Comment on a book she is reading.
- Join a Bible study and introduce yourself.
- Open a door for her.

was an answer to prayer. It changed my whole week and grew our relationship.

- Just check in to say, "Hi, how are you?" and really listen. It doesn't have to be complicated. The simple act of listening can change everything.
- If she shares something challenging with you, ask if she needs a hug—and if so, give her a great one!
- Celebrate each other's little-by-little progress or big leaps.
- Grab a box of popsicles, a watermelon, or a basket of peaches and spend intentional time telling your friend all the things you are proud of her for.
- Celebrate "friend-iversaries," answered prayers, and courage. Celebrate what you want to see more of!

CULTIVATE IT

Circle some ideas that might work for your particular life situation, and do one of them now. Flag this page, and remember the rest of these ideas for later, when these opportunities present themselves. When they do, you'll be ready to take the leap and plant one of these seeds to grow a fruitful friendship!

Surround yourself with friends who are traveling the path you want to take. For me, that has meant soaking myself in local friendships (despite fears of mess and imperfections!), intentionally getting to know our neighbors, and spending time with church family outside the walls of the church building, just enjoying being together. Last night twenty of us descended on a local Chick-fil-A for milkshakes and great conversation. It was simple and so good. It doesn't have to be complicated. Just get with people and let God do the rest.

Pray with me:
    God, help us find ways to cultivate community and step out in faith to take the first steps to making friends, amen.

CHOOSE COMMUNITY OVER COMPARISON

One early morning, when Grace was still a baby, I got bored of my usual morning walk route. So I took Grace's stroller off the beaten path, across the street to the retirement community near our house. We were a bit of an odd sight—a thirtysomething redhead with a baby in tow. Would they think we were intruding?

Instead of being met by suspicion, we were greeted with joy. "Oh my soul, it's so good to see some young people around here!" "Look at that beautiful baby! It's so refreshing to see you walk in this neighborhood!" "Well, isn't that a sight!" The silver-haired residents stopped us to chat. Grace and I were thrilled by the encounter, and I decided to walk by their community on a regular basis. Four years and two strollers later, I still take the kids on a daily walk past the retirement community. The residents have become our dear friends. Mr. John and Mrs. Alice, Ms. Rhetta, Jim Ward, Shirley, Mr. Bill, and many more are now woven into the fabric of our lives.

We do much more than exercise on our morning adventures. We cultivate memories and manners on our walks. Gracie practices her "Good mornings" while intentionally looking in the eyes of our friends, and the babies smile and coo at the extra attention. The elderly residents love Grace's enthusiasm, and she enjoys their happy responses. We observe patience in the pace of fellow walkers and kindness in how they genuinely look out for one another. Mr. Bill goes from house to house each morning, moving the newspapers from the end of the driveways to each resident's doorstep.

We cultivate passion for the outdoors as we listen for birds and hear woodpeckers. We spot new flowers growing, and I name various plant types and trees for her. We often collect a few things along the way: dandelions, acorns, "whirlydos" (maple seeds), and special rocks.

We eventually make our way to the highlight of our path: the community garden. Our silver-haired friends know how to grow things! Their shared garden is filled with dozens of raised garden plots, each with its own unique personality and wisdom. Hazel uses old pantyhose to tie her tomatoes to their stakes. John takes empty plastic soda bottles, cuts them in half, and puts the spout end into the ground, making a watering hole to get nutrients close to the roots. Mr. B carefully marks his lettuce varieties with paint sticks. There are very few newfangled gardening contraptions here; these seasoned gardeners know they just need what works—nothing fancy.

They don't compare their gardens—who has the latest stuff or the biggest harvest. They learn and grow and encourage together. If Hazel is sick, the others tend her plot. If Jeane is on a trip to see her grandkids, they water her rhubarb and butter beans. When Cliff is having a rough day with his arthritis, Mitch checks on his blueberry bushes and brings him the day's harvest.

They take care of one another. That's what community is all about: helping each other keep our unique gardens flourishing.

We all have different garden plots and different ways of growing things, yet we all keep growing as long as we do it together. We savor and share the harvest with everyone. We celebrate together, because our fruit was harvested *together*.

COMPARISON KILLS COMMUNITY

Comparison is the greatest killer of togetherness.

I struggle with this. Just today I caught myself thinking, *She's doing it better than I am.*

But you know what? She should be. Because she's doing her "it," and I need to focus on doing mine. We each have been given a unique assignment on this earth—a garden plot all our own. And our garden plots were intentionally put in the same community garden—not isolated or alone. Our lives together tell a bigger story than we can see. We were created for community. We were created to cultivate together and share the harvest with others.

CULTIVATE IT

In the following list, circle or mark the lies that you've believed or that you are struggling with now. If you've experienced all of these, don't hesitate to draw a giant circle around this whole list! Let's call the lies what they are and mark them boldly. On the other side of naming the lies is seeing the truth.

We believe a lot of lies, don't we? Here are just a few examples:

- I'm not as _____ as she is.
- I don't have what she has.
- I don't have it all together.
- I don't look like her.
- I'm not as organized.
- I'm not as talented.
- I'm not superwoman.
- How does she do it all?
- She's more spiritually advanced than I am.
- She's younger than I am and is doing more.
- She understands the Bible better than I do.
- I'm not as outgoing.
- She's already doing my idea.
- I'm not as important.
- She doesn't yell at her kids like I do.
- She has more energy than I do.
- I'm not as thin, fit, or confident.
- She has a bigger house.
- Her life is more valuable because she is more popular.
- Her prayer life is better than mine.
- Her finances are more in order than mine.
- Her spouse is more loving than mine.
- She lives in a better neighborhood.
- Her education level is better.
- Her kids are more behaved.
- She has a tribe, and I need to find my people.

How exactly did we come to these false conclusions? What led us to believe these lies in the first place? Think about it, and try to notice the root of the comparison weed the next time it crops up.

Perhaps it was a social media post, a television show, an advertisement, or a magazine cover that told you that you must have something or be someone in order to be loved, beautiful, healthy, smart, organized, or valuable. In our world, it is hard to guard our hearts from all of these unhealthy influences. We can't live in a bubble, but we can fill our souls with truth to combat the lies when they crop up.

If we saturate our hearts with comparison, we are feeding ourselves poison. Perfection is a man-made chemical that can kill intentional living from the roots up. Let's trade comparison for cultivating together.

CULTIVATE COMMUNITY

Don't wait for community to show up at your door: be the invitation. Ask someone to come over, even if your house is a mess. I don't know about you, but I feel so relieved when I go to someone's house that is perfectly imperfect like mine! Community and connection to God's heart are the rewards of inviting people over, not what people think of us.

Fruitful friendships are worth embracing awkward for.

Fruitful friendships allow us to celebrate our imperfections together.

Fruitful friendship overlooks your broken fence and admires your garden.

Fruitful friendships point us to God's heart.

Fruitful friendship is possible.

Cultivators embrace AWKWARD and grow in community.

CULTIVATE

SEEDS OF GRACE AND TRUTH

We need meaningful relationships to grow what matters.

The lies of perfection try to hold us back from making
any connections at all. You don't have to be perfect
to grow fruitful relationships. Being vulnerable in
our flaws is the very thing that connects us.

Fruitful friendships grow not because we don't experience
fear, but because breaking ground on meaningful
relationships becomes more important than our fear.

Fruitful friendship is patient, imperfect, forgiving, humble,
encouraging, truthful, trusting, and grace filled.

Fruitful friendship embraces awkward
and asks a second question.

Jesus didn't have a megaphone or an Instagram
account. He had two feet and one goal. Little by
little, person by person, He changed all of history.

Good friends overlook your broken
fence and admire your garden.

GRACE FROM THE GARDEN

Garden Markers

Flowers spring up where friends have walked.

—UNKNOWN

Garden markers are a necessary part of any garden that has more than a few plants—especially if you are growing anything from seed. I made the mistake of not marking my plants one season. Ari lovingly picked, sliced, and served a beautiful red pepper to Grace thinking it was a sweet bell. It was not. To this day, Grace emphatically reminds us that she *does not like spicy peppers* every time a vegetable lands on her plate.

Lesson learned.

Mark your plants.

You can make garden markers out of paint stirrers, buy ceramic ones from garden stores, or take a paint pen and write on rocks or sticks. There are dozens of ways to do it.

This year we wanted to do something that was both practical and meaningful.

Our garden became quite a destination after Sarah was born. Friends would come over and ask two things: How were we doing with two babies, and how was Gracie's Garden? Garden tours became as regular as fireflies in July.

As our family has grown, so has our garden over the years. We now have forty feet of raised garden bed space, an array of various pots and planters, and the flower beds that my mom gifted to us when Joshua was born. As you can tell by the metaphors in this book, we sort of like this gardening thing. If there's dirt, something gets planted in it! We have eighty-eight unique species planted in our veggie and flower beds this season.

Count the varieties of plants in your own yard, if you have one, and you'll be surprised at the number of things growing. Add a love for cultivating to the mix, and a helpful little red-headed garden buddy, and you may end up with as many varieties as we have!

I got to thinking about all the people who loved on us after we welcomed Sarah, and I decided to honor them in a unique way. We named each of our plants after these special friends, pairing each plant with one of the wonderful people who filled our lives with love this year.

Our personalized garden markers include:

- Walter's Mustard
- John's Sir-Crunch-a-Lot Cucumbers
- Rachel's Hula Berry Strawberries
- Jackie's Sugar Baby Watermelons
- Marcia's Black Beauty Zucchini
- Ester's Nagami Kumquat
- Kate's Chamomile
- Jamie's Forget-Me-Nots
- Aunt Kathy's Bee Balm

- Nancy's Cut-and-Come-Again Zinnias
- Winny's Collarette Cosmos
- Mrs. Lorraine's Profusion White Zinnias
- Kristy's Pink Popsocks Cosmos

The garden markers were a hit! We sent photos to each of our friends to show them the special place they had in Gracie's Garden that season. As we tended to each plant, we thought of the community God had grown in our lives, and it made the garden come alive with meaning! Our garden markers sing to us a constant song: *love grows here.*

CHAPTER 10

....

PRESERVE THE FRUIT

LIE: the PAST isn't valuable;
it's all about the FUTURE.

TRUTH: Remembering God's FAITHFULNESS
helps us cultivate a meaningful legacy.

Grace's fingers were sticky with peach nectar—a marvelous golden mess—as she nibbled on our ingredients. We sat in my mom's kitchen, watching her do what generations have done before her in our family: preserve the good stuff. The peaches from our tree brought back memories of Alabama road trips when I was a kid. My little brother and I would sit on the porch at Peach Park and lick clean our bowls of vanilla ice cream topped with Chilton County peaches.

Fruit, by its nature, begins to spoil the moment it is harvested. But the arts of preserving and canning allow us to enjoy the harvest later. We don't have to consume the harvest right away but can preserve some for another use—when winter turns fields to clay, when crops are low, or when you need a taste of summer during a rough season.

Mom was filling so much more than peaches into those Mason jars that day. She was filling them with history, tradition, and love.

MARKING THE MEANINGFUL

The good stuff of life is much like our prized jams and the sweet fruit we harvest. The taste of peach preserves on a fresh biscuit can make even the harshest of winters feel warm. Preserving the good stuff is the act of marking the meaningful. It's seeing the fruit that God has grown in your life and doing something with it—perhaps to be enjoyed later by you or generations after you.

Memories made and preserved through photographs, written words, a box of love letters, worn and filled journals, special mementos from adventures together, and stories told and passed down—these treasures brought out from the shelf during dry seasons of the soul can change everything. They help you to remember.

Because it's easy to forget when the land freezes over again in winter.

It's easy to forget the little by little and the joy of the journey.

It's easy to forget God's faithfulness in the harvest and how He has provided for you.

Preserving what matters means intentionally remembering.

REMEMBER

Remember is a word God loves. He used it 166 times in the Bible to encourage us to preserve the good stuff. Here are just a few examples:

> You shall *remember* that you were a slave in the land of Egypt, and the LORD your God brought you out from there with a mighty hand and an outstretched arm. (Deuteronomy 5:15)

> *Remember* the wondrous works that [God] has done,
> his miracles and the judgments he uttered.
> (1 Chronicles 16:12)

> I will *remember* the deeds of the LORD;
> yes, I will *remember* your wonders of old.
> (Psalm 77:11)

Lately, I've been feeling God speaking these remembrances over me:

Lara, remember the miracle of Ari's faith! Remember how I changed Ari's heart and made it completely new.

Remember the miracle of how I healed your marriage. Remember all the pain you experienced when you tried to live without Me, and the peace and joy you and Ari both have now as you've committed your hearts to Me. You are free.

Remember the months and months of waiting for another baby. I was opening your heart. Remember the day that Joshua was born. I make all things new in My time.

Remember how I blessed you with Sarah's life and deep-ened your faith as you stepped into the unknown. Remember the expansive love for her I cultivated in you little by little, in My perfect timing.

Remember how good things came out of hard things and how I showed you in it all what truly matters. Remember the harvest of contentment that followed your time of being broken.

Do not forget how I have changed you—taking you from the dark to the light.

Remember, Lara. To everything there is a season and a perfect time under heaven.

Remember.

I never could have predicted the plans God had for our family or the things He would ask us to step into. If God would have told me any of these plans, I would have laughed and said, "No way!" I wouldn't have thought we would have the capacity or faith for some of what He led us into.

God knew.

His plan was to stretch us and grow our faith so that we would rely on Him to be our strength through this journey. He wanted to break us down to build us back up again, new and changed. His plan was to take us through long seasons of "not yet" and "wait." His plan was to prune and ripen us for something better than we could have imagined.

He was cultivating our souls and lives for His great plan.

And He has a plan for you too.

CULTIVATE IT

In what ways has God been faithful in your life? What do you want to preserve and remember? What are you "putting up" in your remembrances for the seasons ahead?

HERE I RAISE MY EBENEZER

In 1 Samuel, we learn that God helped His people win a great victory, and to commemorate this, "Samuel took a stone and set it up between Mizpah and Shen. He named it Ebenezer, saying, 'Thus far the LORD has helped us'" (1 Sam. 7:12 NIV). Ebenezer means "stone of help." Every time an Israelite saw the stone, he would have a tangible reminder of the Lord's power and faithfulness.

I recently made an Ebenezer wall in our home. I chose several photographs from the most pivotal moments in our faith and times God grew life-altering fruit in our lives:

- the days of each of our children's births,
- a recent photograph of our whole family together—stronger after having gone through this season of refining, and
- a photo of us with Sarah's brave and selfless birth mom.

In these photographs, not selected for outward beauty but for inward transformation by God's grace, we remember. They all bring us right back to what matters and point us forward with greater confidence—knowing Who our helper and provider is. In these Ebenezers, when times are hard, we have preserved a reconnection to what matters.

The song "Come, Thou Fount of Every Blessing" has been pouring out of my lips as I've written this chapter to you:

> Come, Thou Fount of every blessing,
> Tune my heart to sing Thy grace;
> Streams of mercy, never ceasing,

> Call for songs of loudest praise.
> Teach me some melodious sonnet,
> Sung by flaming tongues above.
> Praise the mount! I'm fixed upon it,
> Mount of Thy redeeming love.

And these last few lines never cease to turn into worship as I sing them! This is our story. Our song.

> Here I raise mine Ebenezer;
> Hither by Thy help I'm come;
> And I hope, by Thy good pleasure,
> Safely to arrive at home.

Pray with me:

God, help us intentionally remember the many ways You have helped us and mark Your faithfulness with meaningful Ebenezers. May these special remembrances help cultivate our faith as we continue to trust in Your power and faithfulness, amen.

SIMPLE REMINDERS

The tradition of "putting up" peaches is as rich as the ritual of picking them. Our family's jam recipe, never written down, has been passed on from my grandmother and my mother—and now to me. Preserving doesn't require anything fancy or too difficult to procure. Just the simplest ingredients—sweet fruit, sugar, and lemon juice—are in the jar.

The ways we preserve and remember the fruit God has

grown in our lives don't need to be complicated or perfect. Many times, simple ingredients are the best ingredients.

CULTIVATE IT

Here are some ideas for practical ways you can preserve what God has grown in your life:

- Having photographs printed and hung on your wall instead of stored on your phone
- Keeping a blessings jar in your kitchen to fill with notes about what you are grateful for
- Writing in the margins of a family Bible
- Placing a small "Ebenezer stone" in a bowl—or in your own garden—for each milestone or miracle you want to remember
- Making art
- Journaling (remember, it can be messy!)
- Planting a blessings garden—one seed or plant for each blessing God has grown in your life
- Writing letters of gratitude and placing them in a special box
- Creating a simple notebook or binder to record the ways God is cultivating your heart or your family's hearts
- Cultivating meaningful holidays and traditions that allow you to celebrate His faithfulness from year to year.

This year Grace and I decided to press flowers from the garden and from special milestones. We collected pansies in the spring from our morning walks to the community garden. We collected cherry blossoms and dandelions on the way to the neighborhood park. After Sarah was born, a friend brought us a beautiful arrangement of purple tulips and lilac, and my great-grandmother Irene's jonquils bloomed that same week. We found four-leaf clovers in March, and peach rose petals from our front yard bushes in April. A friend brought over hydrangea blooms and a hug during a week she knew I needed some extra encouragement. In the summer, the zinnias begged us to harvest their colorful petals and press them in Bibles, cookbooks, catalogs, and any book we could find. We pressed these petals and blooms little by little, and when the heat of August drew us inside, we arranged them all on a big canvas for our home. A little Mod Podge sealed up our garden treasures, and our project was complete. It is a glorious reminder that though some seasons brought hardship, God was ever faithful.

We all go through various seasons in our lives—times of great bounty and times of inward focus. There are times when our gardens are bursting with blooms and times when we aren't sure if spring will ever come again.

Spring always follows winter. But in the meantime, we store up the good of spring to remind us of what we have learned and to give us hope for when the winter comes.

And preserving the good stuff doesn't just mean preserving what has passed; it means celebrating what is to come. When you make jam, you are preparing enjoyment in a jar for the future. You're preserving and preparing hope.

> One generation shall commend your works to another,
> and shall declare your mighty acts.
>
> —PSALM 145:4

PLANT SEEDS OF LEGACY

I've written and deleted this sentence to you many times over in the last five minutes. I can't find adequate words to tell you about what is resting to the left of my keyboard.

I have been saving it for a day when I could savor it well—a day with lots of margin and quiet in the house. But my perfect time slot hasn't arrived yet. Grace is singing at the top of her lungs downstairs, and I only have a few minutes to myself. So instead of waiting for perfect, I'm making a decision to cultivate an intentional life with what I have, right where I am.

The fragile, well-worn book is wrapped in a thick plastic cover to protect it. There are notes and aged ribbons peeking out from the pages. Memories, stories, and lives were shaped by these thin, gold-rimmed sheets of my grandpa's Bible. The gold is barely a whisper now, though—a reminder that the words inside, not the outer shell, are all that lasts.

I feel hesitant to open it, fearful that I may not be able to contain my emotions.

I know the end of this story. And it's a good one.

I know the people who were changed by these pages. They changed me forever.

Cecil and Celeste.

Oh, hello, tears. I was expecting you.

Opening the protective covering, I smell the home they shared together in the lingering scent of sweet coffee, worn carpet, and garden roses. I remember the chorus of African violets Grandma loved to tend by the kitchen window, playing catch with my cousins in the backyard, and their wedding photo proudly displayed in the front entrance of their modest home.

The book is heavy and the leather is worn. I rewind back

to when Celeste might have chosen this particular Bible for Cecil—a large-print King James Version. She knew how much he loved to read and how his eyes were starting to tire, even at the age of forty-nine.

The inside flap reads:

Cecil C. Austin
A Christmas gift
From my dear wife
December 25, 1964

Cecil loved his wife and this gift. What Celeste didn't know at the time, though, was that this Bible would someday turn into a gift for her. Cecil would live another thirty-seven years, poring through the pages, writing notes to her in the margins along the way. I think somehow he knew he would meet his Maker first. He sowed little bits of heaven into her soul with every note he penned in these pages.

Perhaps Cecil knew that his granddaughter might open this book one day, too, looking for wisdom. He knew one thing for sure: whoever opened this book would find life here.

I imagine my grandma holding this Bible in her hands, remembering her sweet husband bringing her wildflowers with her morning coffee. I imagine her missing him after he passed and coming back here, to his Bible, to sense his presence and remember the joy they shared together.

In the pages of this Bible, Cecil preserved for his bride what he'd learned about cultivating an intentional life, dotted with encouragement and love notes along the way. He had the forethought to know what she would need after he was gone. He loved her when they were together on this earth, and he preserved that love in this precious Bible to help her in the future.

In the same way, we are given gifts to turn right back around to the world—helping them see the path forward.

> Each of you should use whatever gift you have received to serve others, as faithful stewards of God's grace in its various forms.
>
> —1 PETER 4:10 NIV

KNOWING THE WAY HOME

I often forget the good things that have happened and focus on what's hard or undone. I forget that I don't have to be perfect. I forget the way home. In the thick of the mess, I want to hold something in my hands that brings me right back to what matters too.

I want Grace, Josh, and Sarah to know the way home, long after Ari and I are gone. There's a pit in my stomach thinking about it because *I love them so much*, and I don't want to imagine not being with them. But the truth is I'm going to leave this earth one day. Ari will too. It's a hard truth to hold in my hands, but it's potentially the most life-giving seed we can plant, friend. It's the seed of legacy.

I want to cultivate truth in my children. I want to equip them to plant their own gardens in this world and learn how to thrive God's way. I want to cultivate a life that is focused on growing what will last longer than I will—not what seems exciting or enticing right this second.

What am I cultivating now that preserves God's faithfulness for my own future encouragement, for my husband and children, and for all those who will live after I'm gone? Like love notes in the margins of Cecil's Bible, the good things we grow with God have the potential to point people home.

Cultivators PRESERVE what matters for future SEASONS, and future GENERATIONS.

SEEDS OF GRACE AND TRUTH

It's easy to forget God's faithfulness in the harvest and how He has provided for you.

Preserving what matters means intentionally remembering.

Remembering God's faithfulness helps us cultivate a meaningful legacy.

A cultivated life is an intentionally prepared life. Prepare meaningful traditions and Ebenezers to celebrate what God has done in your life, and watch your faith grow!

Preserving doesn't require anything fancy or too difficult to procure. Just the simplest ingredients—sweet fruit, sugar, and lemon juice—are in the jar. The ways we preserve and remember the fruit God has grown in our lives don't need to be complicated or perfect either.

Here I raise mine Ebenezer;
Hither by Thy help I'm come;

And I hope, by Thy good pleasure,
Safely to arrive at home.

We are given gifts to turn right back around to the world—
helping them see the path forward. The good things we grow
with God have the potential to point people home.

GRACE FROM THE GARDEN

The Day I Thought I Would Lose the Garden

We come from the earth. We return to the
earth. And in between we garden.

—AUTHOR UNKNOWN

One of the thrills of the garden for me is adding fresh herbs to family meals. Even if I pick up a rotisserie chicken from the grocery store, running out in my bare feet to clip a few rosemary and thyme sprigs makes our meal come to life.

One night, however, while adding fresh pineapple sage and lemon juice to broiling fish in the oven, the glass dish exploded. So did the tears for me.

It had been a particularly challenging day already. That morning I had found out there were termites in our raised garden beds. The exterminator told me that everything would have to be removed and destroyed—the wood frames, the mulch, and even some of the plants and soil. Everything had been growing so well. All the weathered cedar frames in which years of memories had grown would all have to be burned.

Ari hugged me, offered to microwave the leftovers in the

fridge, and said, "Lara, you are worth more than dinner. I know you worked hard to make this meal, and that this has been a hard day, but making a beautiful dinner is not what God values in you most." He was right.

We couldn't afford to replace the whole garden, nor did I have the time to start over. My friend Renee offered to drive all the way from Charlotte to help me transfer all the plants to baby pools if we had to. My neighbor Tori offered to dive into the baby pool plan too. But I was still in denial. So I had tried making an unusually fancy dinner to drown my sorrows.

As Ari held me close with words of truth and love, an old hymn came to mind: "This world is not my home. I'm just a'passin' through."

When things feel like they are falling apart, it leaves me craving what never fades. God knew this would be the lesson I needed. When I finally came to terms with the new company we had in the garden, and let God's lesson take root, hope and peace flooded in.

We prayed and researched and came up with a plan, knowing that this plan could fail and that would ultimately be okay too. We replaced the wood chip mulch (termite food) around the garden beds with river rocks and decided to see if that might be enough to keep them from multiplying. After a couple of weeks, the termites were somewhat miraculously gone! My old cedar wood frames still remain—with a few extra holes, but we don't mind. Not a single plant was harmed, and the baby pool can continue being filled with sweet bare-bum babies in the summer instead of sweet potatoes and turnips.

Now I look at the garden a little differently—with open hands for whatever God has planned. Someday Gracie's Garden will fade, but the love grown here will, Lord willing, remain.

A NEW SEASON

The winter season is upon us, and I take a deep breath. As the temperature drops, I cozy up with little Josh in the armchair by the garden window while Sarah naps and Gracie plays. I look out at the still-green garden plot and remember the suede brown earth sprouting new life in spring, the green glory of summer, and the blaze of color in autumn. I remember the company kept and fruitful friendships grown. I remember the tiny seeds we planted months ago, and how they grew little by little—from seed to awkward sprout to blooming and bountiful plant. Despite the mistakes made and imperfections, my little garden was more than I could have asked for or imagined—far better than I had planned.

A chill from the crack in the windowsill makes its way to my cheek. A pang of sadness hits me as I realize the first hard freeze of the season is coming. Letting go is hard—a little death—but it's time. It's time, once again, to give thanks and surrender to the next season.

COMING HOME TO THE GARDEN

In the morning, I wake to a sad sight: drooping tomato vines, zapped from the cold. A reminder that nothing on this earth lasts forever. The annuals return to the ground, and though the soil remains, it's ever changing based on what I planted that year—whatever the roots left behind.

Pulling things out after the first hard freeze is stingless, though. I wouldn't want the seasons any other way. I enter into the season of winter once more, knowing and trusting that after winter always comes spring.

I could look out at this patch of white snow and see emptiness, or I could see what I know to be true after spending time in the garden: hope.

In winter, I stare out at the bare garden and I dream in petals and vines, color and creatures, plants enjoyed at our dinner table and flowers enjoyed by the bees. I know that winter won't last forever, and as much as I love this special place, it won't last forever either. As I was reminded the day I thought I would lose the garden, the flowers fade. Our stuff and our accomplishments won't last. Even the good things built here on this earth won't last. The only thing that lasts is His love.

So now faith, hope, and love abide, these three; but the greatest of these is love.

—1 CORINTHIANS 13:13

ETERNAL IMPACT

I can't stop thinking about eternal impact. About how our seemingly small actions influence our children and everyone we know.

Opening our homes.

Seeking to understand and love the company kept in the garden and in our lives.

Choosing to ask a second question instead of keeping conversation surface-level.

Getting our hands dirty in the soil—hands and heart undistracted.

Praying for friends in the way you'd want to be prayed for: Passionately. Generously. Fervently. No perfect words required. Perfect words don't matter—your surrendered heart does.

Celebrating sprouting seeds, golden yellow weeds, and everything in between.

Rejoicing in our weakness.

And receiving God's limitless grace during the many, many, many times we mess up.

We don't have to be perfect to cultivate an intentional life and help generations after us learn to do the same. The times I mess up, get to say I'm sorry, or tell our children about how I'm struggling and trying to rely on God in my weakness, those are gifts. Imperfection is a gift because it opens a door for us to see His ever-present grace. Right where we are, in every season, His grace abounds. Eternal impact comes from a heart cultivated with His essential grace—a heart set on eternity. We know where we're going—and it's good.

As the seasons have changed once more, I feel profound gratitude. Writing these words to you, and living out these pages, has been both refining and hard. But, my fellow Cultivator, you know the secret now. Out of hard things come good things.

Thank You, Father.

Thank You.

I'm grateful for another day to plant good seeds in the hearts of my children and for the truth that we can't take anything in this life to heaven with us. Not a thing. That encourages me to plant things here on earth that last longer than I will. I hope it encourages you too.

CULTIVATE WHAT MATTERS

New life starts with a tiny seed, which must let go of its shell to sprout.

There is power—energy, ability, great potential—hiding in each one.

The magic is already inside. You just have to cultivate it.

Begin today. Little by little—and with bold leaps of faith— clear the weeds, plant good seeds, and tend to them with fierce devotion.

There is a great harvest waiting for you at the end—and in the in-between.

> Blessed is the man who trusts in the LORD,
>   whose trust is the LORD.
> He is like a tree planted by water,
>   that sends out its roots by the stream,
> and does not fear when heat comes,
>   for its leaves remain green,
> and is not anxious in the year of drought,
>   for it does not cease to bear fruit.
>
> —JEREMIAH 17:7-8

CULTIVATE TOGETHER GUIDE

*Friends overlook your broken fence
and admire your GARDEN.*

Why on earth do many seed packets—the sort you'd find at your local grocer or hardware store—contain hundreds of seeds? This has always baffled me. I'm all for a great value, but I do not need to plant two hundred carrots in any given season. We are a carrot-loving family, but even two dozen homegrown carrots can be hard to find homes for. We snack, we bake, we pickle, we preserve, and there are still leftovers. Sure, some seeds can be saved and planted the following year, but I am four years into my pack of Danvers 126 seeds, and nowhere near finishing! Farmer friends, you may be laughing at this question given your seed quantity needs, but for me, the average gardener, I require only two dozen or so.

So what do you do with seed surplus? Wouldn't it be wonderful to get together with a group of fellow cultivators and exchange them with one another? That's exactly what gardeners have been doing for decades, passing on heirloom varieties and gardening wisdom.

Welcome to your seed exchange, friends. I created this Cultivate Together Guide to help you exchange meaningful conversation, encouragement, and the good seeds of what God is doing in your lives. We were all given a surplus of blessings to pass along to others. We need fellow cultivators to encourage us in dry times and help us see and celebrate progress. My prayer is that these discussion questions will grow your friendships and your faith!

Whether you're doing this study in a group, with a friend, or on your own, this discussion guide gives you a chance to think about what you've learned from *Cultivate* and make it your own.

Here are a few helpful tips to get you started.

- Listen as people share their doubts. Validate their questions. Practice giving one another room to grow and express feelings and fears.
- Shared trust is built when we commit to keeping personal stories confidential. When talking about cultivating what matters in our lives, personal information is bound to come up. Love one another well by keeping everything within the group.
- Pray for the group and your time together. It's helpful to pray when you are together, and in the in-between. Ask God to help each of you understand and retain what is learned and discussed—and to give you the boldness to share what you learn as He gives you opportunities. Prayer changes things.
- Practice the fruitful friendship tips from chapter 9 in your discussions together: ask second questions, listen below the surface, and embrace awkward.

- I've given you ten discussion questions for each chapter. Feel free to use them all, or focus on just a few if you have a larger group. I'm excited for you!

CHAPTER 1: CULTIVATE WHAT MATTERS

Before the group discussion, identify and write out your favorite takeaway from this chapter:

_____

_____

DISCUSSION QUESTIONS:

1. In what ways have you been believing the lie that you have to do it all?
2. What is one thing you want to cultivate in your life? (Review the list on p. 23 for ideas.) Imagine what your life would look like if you were to cultivate what matters most to you. What would be different in your life? How would you feel? How would growing what matters affect the people around you?
3. What words or images come to mind when you think of the word *cultivate*? What appeals to you about the possibility of becoming a *cultivator* of your life?
4. Consider the following statement: "A cultivated life is made richer because of our flaws and failures. I've learned far more from my mistakes than any of my successes, and I've gained courage and confidence from seasons of challenge." Do you agree or disagree? Why?
5. Think of one person you know who, like Grandpa Cecil,

lived a cultivated, intentional life. What appeals to you about his or her life? What aspects of that person's life do you want to emulate?

6. Have you ever chosen fear over faith? Describe the situation. What possibility are you holding on to right now, like opening a packet of tiny seeds and deciding whether or not to plant them?

7. Describe a time when you chose not to do something that you really wanted to do because you didn't want to "get messy," like gardening in white pants.

8. Consider the following statement: "The garden begs for my presence, and when I give it, it grows." In what areas of your life are you fully present right now? In what areas are you missing the joy of being fully present— undistracted, unafraid, and willing to get dirty and do hard work?

9. Do you ever tend to think you can handle more than you truly can and end up with too many plants in your life's garden? Why or why not?

10. Discuss the following statement: "A powerful fertilizer to nourish the things that truly matter in life is the word *no.*" Do you agree or disagree? Why?

After the discussion time, identify the first action step you'll take related to all you've just learned and discussed. One small step forward is all you need to start growing!

My first starting step this week:

_____

_____

_____

CHAPTER 2: EMBRACE YOUR SEASON

Before the group discussion, identify and write out your favorite takeaway from this chapter:

_____

_____

Write out the little-by-little progress you made since the last meeting, or how it felt to do your one starting step from the previous chapter:

_____

_____

DISCUSSION QUESTIONS:

1. Describe a time when your circumstances seemed bleak and you felt hopeless. What were your emotions at that time? How did that situation affect your relationship with God?

2. In retrospect, in what ways do you think God was using your pain to transform your heart and life under the surface, like a seed soaking up nutrients under the ground that will eventually help it to sprout?

3. Look over the descriptions of various seasons on pages 46–47. What season do you think you are in right now?

4. How does understanding your life's season equip you on your journey to cultivate an intentional life?

5. "The seasons teach us how to do life well, revealing a life-giving rhythm: we flourish through intentional periods of stillness, growth, hard work, and rest. We need this

rhythm in our days, in our weeks, and in our seasons." What rhythms do you want to cultivate in your days, weeks, and years?

6. Have you ever believed the lies that you can't move forward because you don't know enough, haven't done enough, or are too messed up? How has this chapter positively altered your perspective of yourself and growing an intentional life?

7. What feelings have you been fighting in your current season? Share your answers from page 53, where you were asked to fill in these blanks: *I feel* _____, *but I know/want to know* _____. Identify a verse or selection of Scripture to go with your answer.

8. Briefly describe some of the seasons you've gone through in your life that have shaped who you are. What did these seasons teach you?

9. Have you felt tension in various seasons? Describe how you felt.

10. Close your time together by practicing saying, "Amen, Lord, let it be" in your current season. Go around the group and offer short prayers of gratitude for the season you're in, and ask God for wisdom and guidance to embrace where He has placed you.

After the discussion time, identify the first action step you'll take related to all you've just learned and discussed. My first starting step this week:

_____

_____

CHAPTER 3: DREAM LIKE A GARDENER

Before the group discussion, identify and write out your favorite takeaway from this chapter:

_____

_____

Write out the little-by-little progress you made since the last meeting, or how it felt to do your one starting step from the previous chapter:

_____

_____

DISCUSSION QUESTIONS:

1. Consider the following statement: "Sometimes, allowing ourselves to dream about the future is an exercise in faith." Do you struggle with dreaming and goal setting? Describe how you feel.
2. What does the Bible say about goals? Read Proverbs 21:5 and Philippians 3. Did Jesus Himself and the apostles have goals? Now read James 4:13–15. What do we learn from these verses about how to cultivate the goals God gives us?
3. The lie confronted in this chapter is: "My life needs to look like everyone else's." Describe a time when you believed this lie. What were the results?
4. Do you think it's possible to cultivate an intentional life if you do only what's easy or expected? Explain your answer.

5. Complete the following sentence: "My cultivated life looks like . . ."

6. What did you learn about dreaming like a gardener in this chapter? What are some of the ways that gardeners dream that are different from our culture's perspective?

7. Rate the following influences on a scale of 1 to 10 (with 10 representing the highest influence). How much is your life determined by what your friends are doing? By other people's opinions? By your own concept of perfection? By what you read online? By God and His Word? Write any insights you gain from doing this exercise.

8. "Intentional living happens when we tune out all the distractions and pay attention to truth." Name some of the distractions that have been beckoning for your attention lately. What are some specific ways you can tune out these distractions in order to pay attention to truth and listen for God's guidance?

9. "Open your eyes and heart to the unexpected, because our unique paths, in our unique seasons, aren't always going to fit into an expected framework." What inspiration or ideas do you get from reading about Grandpa Cecil's highway garden? In what ways can you cultivate the seemingly useless areas of your life to be made alive again?

10. Knowing where you want to be one year from now, what do you need to cultivate today?

After the discussion time, identify the first action step you'll take related to all you've just learned and discussed.

My first starting step this week:

_____

_____

_____

CHAPTER 4: NOURISH YOUR SOIL

Before the group discussion, identify and write out your favorite takeaway from this chapter:

_____

_____

Write out the little-by-little progress you made since the last meeting, or how it felt to do your one starting step from the previous chapter:

_____

_____

DISCUSSION QUESTIONS:
1. Have you ever been rooted in fear—such as fear of what others thought of you, fear of not being enough, or fear of failure? If so, which word best describes your typical response to those fears: *worry* or *trust*? Why do you think you tend to respond in that way?
2. Say the following sentence out loud: "I am enough in God alone." Do you believe that? Why or why not? "Let the dirt be dirt," and share your honest thoughts.

3. Read Romans 5:8 and Ephesians 2:4–5. What did you learn about God's love and His grace in these verses?

4. "Because of my faith in Christ, I have eternal hope." Do you have the eternal hope of knowing that you will spend eternity in heaven with Christ? Remember to lean into your doubts in order to till up your soil and prepare it for new life. Discuss how you feel, and if your answer is no, seek wisdom from God's Word and trusted faith mentors.

5. Consider the following statement: "Perfect soil doesn't exist. The goal is having *plantable* soil." What images come to mind when you think of "plantable soil"? Describe the character traits of a person who has cultivated "plantable soil" in his or her life.

6. Do you have any boulders of fear and worry, thorns and roots from the past, fruitless striving, or dry soil that is keeping the soil of your life's garden from being plantable? If so, what specific steps can you take to remove those obstacles and let God transform your soil? Remember, keeping the soil of your life healthy is a process, not a destination.

7. What insights have you learned about the importance of good soil when planting a garden? Will a healthy plant grow in unhealthy soil? Why is the soil so important?

8. Read Jesus' parable of the soils in Matthew 13:3–9. Which of the four soils do you think best represents your life right now?

9. What's in your soil right now? Describe three challenges you have struggled with recently (such as comparison, worry, or procrastination).

10. The lie confronted in this chapter is "It's impossible to

start fresh or move forward." Describe a time when you believed this lie.

After the discussion time, identify the first action step you'll take related to all you've just learned and discussed. My first starting step this week:

_____

_____

_____

CHAPTER 5: PLANT YOUR SEEDS

Before the group discussion, identify and write out your favorite takeaway from this chapter:

_____

_____

Write out the little-by-little progress you made since the last meeting, or how it felt to do your one starting step from the previous chapter:

_____

_____

DISCUSSION QUESTIONS:

1. Describe a time when you sensed God calling you to do something that felt outside of your comfort zone or was

231

risky. What was it? How did you respond? What were the results?

2. Consider the following statement: "Growing things is an exercise in optimism. It's expectant hope." Do you agree or disagree? Why?

3. Describe what you learned in this chapter about "a farmer's faith." In what ways do hardworking farmers illustrate optimism and expectant hope? What can we learn from their "leap of faith" each growing season?

4. Read Hebrews 11:1. Has there ever been a time when you believed in something you couldn't yet see? Describe your own "leap of faith."

5. In what ways is cultivating an intentional life a process of "faith in action"?

6. What emotions do you experience when you realize that even when you do plant something, you can't predict exactly how it will grow?

7. Why do you think most of us prefer to have a solid, predictable plan instead of trusting God to work out the details in His own way and on His own time?

8. Describe a time when you realized that "all the titles, recognition, dollars, and seemingly certain things in the world won't satisfy you." What is the only source of true satisfaction in life? Why?

9. Consider this statement: "Prayer isn't just asking for things; it's an act of surrender. We place our worries, fears, dreams, and questions in God's hands and let go. We cultivate trust in the ultimate Cultivator." What are some of your worries, fears, dreams, and questions that you can place in your Cultivator's hands through prayer?

10. When you think of cultivating new things as "planting

seeds," how does this encourage you to take the first small step toward starting? Remember, imperfect progress is still progress. And small steps and time invested will add up!

After the discussion time, identify the first action step you'll take related to all you've just learned and discussed. My first starting step this week:

_____

_____

_____

CHAPTER 6: GROW IN THE WAIT

Before the group discussion, identify and write out your favorite takeaway from this chapter:

_____

_____

Write out the little-by-little progress you made since the last meeting, or how it felt to do your one starting step from the previous chapter:

_____

_____

DISCUSSION QUESTIONS:
1. Describe a time when you had to wait for something in your life.

2. What good things grow through periods of waiting?

3. The lie confronted in this chapter is: "Waiting is not good or productive." Describe a time when you believed this lie. What were the results?

4. Consider the following statement: "Cultivating a garden takes time, and during that time God can prepare and equip us." How does this truth affect your perspective of waiting time?

5. Read Psalm 37:7. What insights did you learn from this verse about waiting?

6. What areas of your life feel awkward or unbalanced right now? Have you been waiting for details in your life to fall into place before you start cultivating?

7. "You can always trust an unknown future to a known and never-changing God." In what ways does knowing God affect your perspective about the future, especially in times of waiting?

8. Have you ever eaten a fruit that wasn't quite ripe yet? What was the flavor like?

9. Why is waiting time necessary for the fruit of our lives' gardens to grow and ripen?

10. "God didn't call us to comfort. He called us to follow Him." Have you ever experienced a time when God asked you to step outside of your comfort zone?

After the discussion time, identify the first action step you'll take related to all you've just learned and discussed. My first starting step this week:

_____

_____

CHAPTER 7: TEND YOUR GARDEN

Before the group discussion, identify and write out your favorite takeaway from this chapter:

_____

_____

Write out the little-by-little progress you made since the last meeting, or how it felt to do your one starting step from the previous chapter:

_____

_____

DISCUSSION QUESTIONS:
1. Name examples of imperfect progress. What can times of slow growth or little-by-little tending teach us?
2. What are some of the dangers of trying to rush good things to develop faster than they should? Consider the example of the roots of fast-growing trees versus slow-growing ones.
3. What is something you have done in the past in an attempt to achieve instant results and a quick fix? Did it work? Why or why not? What is something you have accomplished in the past that took a while to achieve results?
4. Review the example of the hundred-dollar bill on page 133. Which would you have chosen: the hundred-dollar bill or the wait of thirty days to receive $107 billion?
5. Look at the three possible scenarios for why we often

choose instant gratification. Which one do you relate to the most and why?

6. Consider the following statement: "Maybe fast isn't the goal. Maybe cultivating an intentional life means aiming for what happens over time—like the richness of relationships—rather than getting to the finish line." Do you agree or disagree? Why?

7. What role does prayer play in our ability to sense God's leading? What role does prayer play in our willingness to obey God's leading?

8. The lie confronted in this chapter is: "Small steps don't make a difference." Describe a time when you believed this lie.

9. If you haven't yet done it, create a tending list of things you want to care for in your life. What priorities are on your tending list?

10. In what specific ways does your tending list affect the things you put on your schedule, to-do list, or planner? Why is that important?

After the discussion time, identify the first action step you'll take related to all you've just learned and discussed.

My first starting step this week:

_____

_____

_____

CHAPTER 8: HARVEST CONTENTMENT

Before the group discussion, identify and write out your favorite takeaway from this chapter:

_____

_____

Write out the little-by-little progress you made since the last meeting, or how it felt to do your one starting step from the previous chapter:

_____

_____

DISCUSSION QUESTIONS:

1. Describe a time when you unrushed your pace and noticed what was growing in your life. What were the circumstances? What emotions did you experience as you savored the moment you were in?
2. What do you complain about most in life? What are some of the specific phrases you use?
3. Consider the following statement: "Ignoring our pain doesn't help us move past it." Why is it unhealthy to bury your complaints and pretend they don't exist?
4. What do your complaints reveal to you? What lies have you been believing?
5. The lie confronted in this chapter is: "I will be content when I have it all." Describe a time when you believed this lie. What were the results?

6. Why do you think contentment is so difficult to cultivate in our society?

7. What are some of the things you have to do in your life right now? Consider responsibilities at home, work, church, your community, your family, and so on. Now rephrase your answers to start with "I get to . . ." instead of "I have to . . ." How does this simple shift of perspective affect your attitude toward your life?

8. Why do you think that prayer—even simple, imperfect prayer—cultivates gratitude in our hearts?

9. What are some of the things you miss in your life when you are distracted by your phone or electronics?

10. Make a list of at least ten things you are grateful for, whether big or small. Be specific!

After the discussion time, identify the first action step you'll take related to all you've just learned and discussed.

My first starting step this week:

_____

_____

_____

CHAPTER 9: FLOURISH WITH OTHERS

Before the group discussion, identify and write out your favorite takeaway from this chapter:

_____

_____

Write out the little-by-little progress you made since the last meeting, or how it felt to do your one starting step from the previous chapter:

_____

_____

DISCUSSION QUESTIONS:

1. The lie confronted in this chapter is: "I can do life by myself." Describe a time when you believed this lie. What were the results?

2. Why is it necessary for us to have friends and cultivate community in our lives? Why can't we do life alone?

3. What would happen to a garden if you encased it in a giant bubble that didn't let anything in or out? Would the garden thrive or die? Why?

4. How does the concept of a garden needing outside influences (pollinators, oxygen, earthworms, and so on) apply to our lives and our relationships with others?

5. Have you ever fallen into the trap of thinking that you had to have only friends who were exactly like you? Why is it also good to have friends who are different from you?

6. True or false: "I have to be perfect, with no flaws, in order to be good at friendship." Explain your answer.

7. Describe a time when you connected to someone more deeply when he or she was honest about flaws and didn't pretend to be perfect.

8. What are some of your fears about friendship? Review the list of fears on pages 186–87. Which of these fears do you identify with? Why?

9. What insights did you gain as you read about the

residents of the retirement community and how they helped one another in their community garden?

10. "Community is the reward of inviting people over, not what people think of us." What emotions do you experience as you realize your house doesn't have to be perfect or your life put together in order to invite people to cultivate community?

After the discussion time, identify the first action step you'll take related to all you've just learned and discussed.

My first starting step this week:

_____

_____

_____

CHAPTER 10: PRESERVE THE FRUIT

Before the group discussion, identify and write out your favorite takeaway from this chapter:

_____

_____

Write out the little-by-little progress you made since the last meeting, or how it felt to do your one starting step from the previous chapter:

_____

_____

DISCUSSION QUESTIONS:

1. Why do you think it is important for us to preserve our stories and pass them down to the next generation?

2. The lie confronted in this chapter is "The past isn't valuable; it's all about the future." Describe a time when you believed this lie. What were the results?

3. What could happen if we stopped preserving what God has done in our lives and no longer passed down these lessons and memories to future generations?

4. Have you ever had a hard time remembering the good in your life and all God has done for you? Describe how you felt.

5. Remembering God's faithfulness is the act of intentionally praising Him for the fruit that has grown in our lives. Name some of the fruit God has grown in your life that you want to remember.

6. What are some specific things you can do to "put up" these memories and store them for the cold winters ahead? What "Ebenezers" can you create in your life?

7. Read Psalm 145:4. Why do you think it is important for one generation to preserve what matters by sharing their experiences and stories about God with the next generation?

8. What seeds of legacy do you want to plant? What can you cultivate for your loved ones, and for all those who will live after you're gone?

9. Read Ephesians 2:8–10. How does God's grace change our view of what a meaningful legacy is?

10. How can we "point people home," helping them find eternal life in Christ?

After the discussion time, identify the first action step you'll take related to all you've just learned and discussed.

My first starting step this week:

_____

_____

_____

CELEBRATE TOGETHER

Now it's time to celebrate all the progress you've made together! For your final discussion time, go around the group and offer words of encouragement to one another and words of gratitude for God's faithfulness! Your words matter. They are seeds planted in your heart and the hearts of others. Choose or create an Ebenezer to help you remember all that God has done on this journey. It doesn't have to be fancy. Some ideas:

- Write an encouraging word or phrase from your journey on a river rock to put in your garden or on your desk.
- Use index cards as "seed packets" and write meaningful words to one another.
- Get mini plants for each person in the group.
- Gather acorns for each person to keep as a reminder that good things grow little by little.
- Press a flower in the pages of this book, or your Bible, to remember your journey together.

I can't wait to follow your journeys! Feel free to share your experiences with the hashtag #CultivateWhatMatters and #TheCultivateBook.

GARDENING 101

Some people calm their stress with a candy
bar; I head off mine with a spading fork.
—A SLENDER ANONYMOUS GARDENER

For my favorite gardening tips and resources, download my
free Cultivate Gardening 101 Guide at LaraCasey.com/
cultivate.

ACKNOWLEDGMENTS

I'm so GRATEFUL!

It's a humbling thing to write a book about the very thing you've experienced while writing it—imperfect progress. Debbie, thank you for your faith, patience, and prayerful support as I wrote and lived out these pages over the last two years. Jennifer and the entire Thomas Nelson team—Meaghan, Lori, Kristi, Jesse, Judy, Kimberly, and Laura—thank you for helping to cultivate *Cultivate*.

To the women I work alongside, Emily, Nicole, Lisa, Amber, Jess, Marissa, Kristin, and Laura, your unwavering support and encouragement as I've written these pages has been a gift from above. Thank you for cultivating what matters alongside me. I praise Him for each of you.

To my literary agent, Claudia, thank you for your wisdom and faithful encouragement.

Em, Gina, Renee, Katelyn, Lysa, Sally, Lindsay, Carrie, Ashlee, Shay, Karen, Cheyenne, Kaitlin, Amber, Nancy, Rhi, Jess, Hayley, Kristin, Erin, Rachel, Kristy, Valerie, Diana, my sister Kathy, and so many friends: thank you for your friendship, and for praying me through this journey. The Lord is faithful.

To the many friends who have joined me for weekly book and life updates online, know that your kindness, letters, and words of encouragement made a difference. Your genuine support mattered.

Jessie and Ashlyn, thank you for praying for these words, and helping me sift through them in the thick of it.

Tori, our morning walks in the neighborhood and your generous friendship helped shape my life and these pages. Thank you.

Talia and Marcia, I praise Him for your faithful examples to me as mothers, wives, and daughters of God. Your prayers and love as I wrote were deeply felt.

To our family group, and my Mama's Group sisters, what a blessing you are to me! Thank you for your love this year!

Walter, you are the bee's knees. Your kindness has made an eternal impact on me, Grace, and more people than you know.

Rhiannon, Jess, Juliette, Megan, Lauren, Rachel, Joslyn, and Sarah Svendsen, thank you for caring for our family so selflessly. I couldn't have written these pages without you!

Mom, Dad, and Stephen, who would have ever thought I'd write a book about gardening? I am so grateful for our family, for Grandpa Cecil and Grandma Bunny, and for all of our trips to Peach Park. And extra-special thanks to you, Mom, for all you planted in our garden and sowed lovingly into our lives.

Ari, this has been my favorite year with you. Thank you for your unwavering faith, for pruning my tomatoes when I couldn't, for migrating the citrus trees each winter, and for your daily prayers for my writing and our lives. I love you.

Gracie, Joshua, Sarah, I love you, little butter beans.

And to Mama J, wherever you are, know that you are loved by a big God who has you in the palm of His hand. Thank you for choosing life for Sarah—we are forever grateful.

P. S. ccgtjhwaesrr ttrry v tg—Love, Joshua Cecil, who is sitting on my lap. (His first published words at the tender age of one.)

She
believed
SHE COULDN'T
so He did.

CONNECT WITH LARA

Online: LaraCasey.com
Instagram: @LaraCasey
Step into Gracie's Garden on Instagram: @GraciesGarden

Join the Community: CultivateWhatMatters.com
@CultivateWhatMatters

ABOUT THE AUTHOR

Hi, y'all! I'm Lara. I'm a mom to three—one through the gift of adoption—a grateful wife, and a believer in the impossible (we have quite the story!). If we were having tea together right now, you'd find out quickly that I'm passionate about helping people get unstuck, unrushed, and living on purpose instead of by accident. To help with those things, I created the PowerSheets grace-filled, goal-setting planner and Write the Word journals, and I founded *Southern Weddings* magazine a decade ago. I'm the author of this little book you're holding in your hands and *Make It Happen: Surrender Your Fear. Take the Leap. Live On Purpose.* I love getting my hands dirty in the garden, exploring local farms, and living in Chapel Hill, North Carolina!

CHOOSE PURPOSE
OVER PERFECT

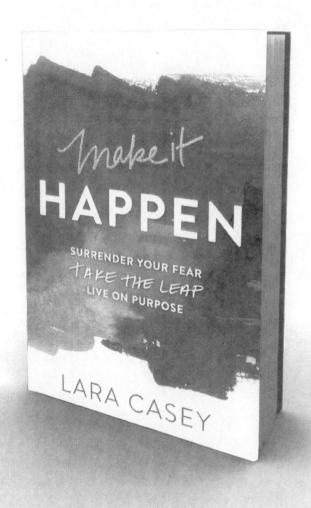